Untethering Educational Leadership

Lingdao, the Chinese word for leadership, is rarely used to denote acts of social persuasion that occur outside of contexts of formal rank or status. However, the ubiquity of informal leadership in China raises a number of practical and theoretical questions.

Based on an analysis of selected Chinese cinematic works depicting settings of educational practice and policy, the book explores how "Western" understandings of leadership emerge from these texts to form discursive media for social change. It also offers a new understanding of *lingdao* and leadership; how they represent a natural human desire, regardless of formal rank or position, to mobilize collective will, change minds, and achieve social change.

The book will be of interest to professional scholars and graduate students of Chinese culture, educational leadership, mass media, and popular culture.

Chenwei Ma is an associate professor of the educational economy and management in Public Administration of Sichuan University. Chenwei is engaged in comparative and international research on education policy.

Roger C. Shouse is a partially retired educator who began work as a high school teacher in 1976. After earning his Ph.D. in 1994 from the University of Chicago, he has served as professor of educational leadership and public administration in the United States and China over the years from 1994 through the present, most recently at Sichuan University

Untethering Educational Leadership

Cases and Contexts from Chinese Cinema

Chenwei Ma and Roger C. Shouse

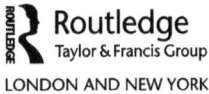
LONDON AND NEW YORK

First published 2024
by Routledge
4 Park Square, Milton Park, Abingdon, Oxon OX14 4RN

and by Routledge
605 Third Avenue, New York, NY 10158

Routledge is an imprint of the Taylor & Francis Group, an informa business

© 2024 Chenwei Ma and Roger C. Shouse

The right of Chenwei Ma and Roger C. Shouse to be identified as authors of this work has been asserted in accordance with sections 77 and 78 of the Copyright, Designs and Patents Act 1988.

All rights reserved. No part of this book may be reprinted or reproduced or utilised in any form or by any electronic, mechanical, or other means, now known or hereafter invented, including photocopying and recording, or in any information storage or retrieval system, without permission in writing from the publishers.

Trademark notice: Product or corporate names may be trademarks or registered trademarks, and are used only for identification and explanation without intent to infringe.

British Library Cataloguing in Publication Data
A catalogue record for this book is available from the British Library

Library of Congress Cataloging in Publication Data
Names: Ma, Chenwei, 1987- author. | Shouse, Roger C., 1954- author.
Title: Untethering educational leadership : cases and contexts from Chinese cinema / Chenwei Ma, Roger C. Shouse.
Identifiers: LCCN 2023047625 (print) | LCCN 2023047626 (ebook) | ISBN 9781032723624 (hardback) | ISBN 9781032723846 (paperback) | ISBN 9781032723778 (ebook)
Subjects: LCSH: Educational leadership--China. | Education in motion pictures--China. | Mass media and education--China.
Classification: LCC LA1133.7 .M3 2024 (print) | LCC LA1133.7 (ebook) | DDC 371.2/011--dc23/eng/20231023
LC record available at https://lccn.loc.gov/2023047625
LC ebook record available at https://lccn.loc.gov/2023047626

ISBN: 978-1-032-72362-4 (hbk)
ISBN: 978-1-032-72384-6 (pbk)
ISBN: 978-1-032-72377-8 (ebk)

DOI: 10.4324/9781032723778

Typeset in Times New Roman
by KnowledgeWorks Global Ltd.

This book is published with financial support from the International Visiting Program for Excellent Young Scholars of Sichuan University.

Contents

List of figures vi
List of tables vii
Preface viii

Introduction 1

1 Impossible mission I: To distinguish the meaning of "leadership" 9

2 Impossible mission II: To depict the film as discursive leadership 20

3 Impossible mission III: To pitch films displaying discursive leadership 40

4 Impossible mission IV: To recognize the discursive leadership through movie lens 55

5 Impossible mission V: To make the familiar new, and the new familiar 96

6 Ongoing mission: Generation-Z, always online! 108

Conclusion 116

Index *121*

Figures

2.1	Relationship between Leadership, Management, Authority and Power	23
2.2	Ideas (A) and Sounds (B) (From Hansen, 2001, Following Saussure, 1916/1959)	33
2.3	Sociolinguistic Negotiation (Time 1)	33
2.4	Sociolinguistic Negotiation (Time 2)	35
6.1	The Usage Rates of We Media among Teens in U.S.	110

Tables

2.1	Intersections of Formality, Leader Type, and Educational Setting	30
3.1	List of Films Depicting Informal Leadership in Chinese Educational Settings	42
3.2	Example of Data Entry for Pretty Big Feet	45
3.3	Varieties of Cinematic Shots – e.g., Pretty Big Feet	46
3.4	Varieties of Angle Shots – e.g., Pretty Big Feet	48
3.5	Use of Lighting Techniques – e.g., Pretty Big Feet	49
3.6	The Creation of Meaning of Films – e.g., Pretty Big Feet	50
3.7	Example of Literature Data Entry – e.g., Pretty Big Feet	52
4.1	Not One Less, Character/Actor Matches	74
5.1	List of Films Depicting Teacher-Student Relationships in Chinese Educational Settings	98
5.2	List of Films Focused on Local Fiscal Status	101
5.3	List of Films Depicted Family Influential Factors	103

Preface

A line from an ancient Chinese poem reads,

"To thoroughly enjoy a thousand-mile sight, climb up another level."*

We, your authors, believe that too few studies of leadership have sought to climb that extra level, to view leadership as a natural human trait displayed throughout the world, over history, and across myriad aspects of human activity. Perhaps we, your authors, have not yet climbed high enough. But then again, there is always more time. Thank you for reading our book.

* From Climbing Stork Tower, Wang Zhihuan, Tang Dynasty poet

Introduction

Orientation

It may seem odd, perhaps folly, to write a book that aims to:

- Propose a concise concept of "leadership."
- Do so in consistent fashion across Chinese and American language and culture
- Advance a new understanding of "educational leadership."
- Tie all the above to the construction of cinematic text, particularly that created by Chinese filmmakers.

This seemingly convoluted task reminds us of a puzzle presented by 16th-century mathematician Gerolamo Cardano. In his classic work, *Ars Magna* (1545), he asks readers to find two numbers with a sum of 10 and product of 40. After a few moments of thought, many readers may conclude that this is impossible. Cardano, however, prefaces his challenge saying, *manifestum est quod casus seu quaestio est impossibilis, sic tamen operabirmus* (which may be translated as "clearly this is impossible, however we will work anyway").[1]

In truth, Cardano's solution involved the introduction of imaginary numbers – e.g., the square root of −1. Though thought to be useless in Cardano's time, such numbers have since been found to have numerous applications across scientific fields (Fierz, 1983). Far from trying to elevate our work to Cardano's level, we simply say that our study also began with a puzzle requiring application of seemingly imaginary ideas that we hope will be found useful across fields of social science, particularly educational leadership.

The puzzle we offer can be expressed in different ways. For example, if Chinese history is replete with stories and cases of common citizens influencing and reshaping social thought and action, why are these rarely if ever linked to the act of *lingdao*, the Mandarin word for "leadership?" Flipping the question, we ask why in America are similar forms of popular social influence *frequently* understood as expressions of "leadership?" To summarize, how do we make sense of a ubiquitous global phenomenon with globally varying semantic interpretation and representation?

Pressing on, we ask whether such variation might narrow inversely with the expansion of social, intellectual, and linguistic interaction between China and the United States? In other words, we raise the possibility of cultural isomorphism with respect to the meaning and labeling of acts of social influence launched by persons and groups outside realms of formal authority. For instance, do we see contemporary signs in China linking forms of informal social influence to the idea of *lingdao*? We note, in fact, the significant number of articles published over the past five years in Chinese journals discussing "western" ideas of informal *lingdao*, particularly within the context of Chinese education and school improvement (Law, 2012; Ma & Shouse, 2019; Shouse & Ma, 2015; Wang & Gao, 2022). As new words and ideas flow through ever-shrinking global social space, can we not begin to imagine *lingdao* and "leadership" as evolving spheres, destined to meld into a more commonly understood concept?

Making this leap of imagination, we suggest that leadership and *lingdao* are natural human tendencies, not bound to formal rank or position. These words signify and represent the capacity of individuals or groups to mobilize social volition; to persuade people to accept ideas or actions which they previously believed were wrong, unnecessary, or irrelevant. In other words, to suspend their own judgment in favor of whomever was attempting to exercise leadership or *lingdao*. This conceptualization does not rule out more specified usages arising out of formal organization ("Principal" is the leader of our school). But it does describe the essential phenomenon, distinguishing it from others such as "management," "rank," "authority," or "power."

We thus arrive at the underlying principle of this book. Whether revealed in voice or action, whether signified as leadership or *lingdao*, a natural disposition toward social change exists within and among individuals and groups. When engaged, this disposition serves as a potential force of influence – a vector, in a field of social space and interaction, influenced, sanctioned, or constrained by structures of formal authority, yet conceptually and empirically distinct from them. Once we accept "leadership" as a natural characteristic of human beings (rather than a function of formal position), we can better grasp why it is that common people – perhaps a church reverend or university librarian – hold potential and capability to "lead" at social levels great and small (Khan et al., 2015).

Still, as suggested by our book's title, we need to weave together this concept of leadership with matters of education and the construction of cinematic text. Starting with the first of these, we argue that although the concept of "educational leadership" has for nearly a century been firmly attached to the management and institutionalization of "brick and mortar" schooling, this no longer need be so. Global urbanization and universalized technology have rendered it increasingly hard to imagine education as a process or endeavor tied to formal institutions, e.g., academic, vocational, military, or religious. Though these remain useful, they exist today within a dense and vast atmosphere of alternative sources of knowledge, teaching, and opportunities for learning. Educational historian Lawrence Cremin (1988) noted, for instance, "...the ubiquitous and incessant education implicit in the very nature of metropolitan life" (p. 9). Cremin's words appeared nearly 40 years ago in his book on American education, an over 700-page tome in which formal schooling is scarcely mentioned.

The validity of Cremin's observation is exponentially evident over the past four decades, though we see its examples long before the 1980s. One could ask, for instance, whether public attitudes about racial justice were changed in the 1950s and 1960s more by classroom lessons or by news broadcasts of civil rights protests – and the often violent opposition toward them. The music of the 1960s contributed to this out-of-school learning; think here of Bob Dylan's *Blowin' in the Wind* or even Frank Zappa's *Trouble Comin' Every Day*. These and other folk songs of social critique not only triggered listener awareness but also echoed into the public square and into schools. *Blowin' in the Wind* becomes not just a global gathering cry in the struggle for peace and justice but also now a popular selection for primary school music classes and holiday concerts. In this book, therefore, we argue that a close connection exists between "leadership" and "education." Both work as social vectors that when sufficiently strong can change minds, behaviors, and public mindscapes.

We thus propose here a concept of "educational leadership" that transcends conventional ties to formal school administration or organizational rank. Educational leadership – *jiaoyu lingdao* – can emerge out of individual or group actions aimed at changing people's thinking and behavior, at either a cognitive/rational or affective/artistic level. These efforts might not be immediately successful. They may not succeed at all (a point to which we shall later return). But such efforts are evident throughout most of the modern world. Humanity is literally surrounded by vectors of educational leadership.

As our book's title highlights, such vectors emerge from the production of cinematic text, which comprises individuals and teams (e.g., producers, writers, directors, technical support) and the narratives they present. Clearly, not all movie productions aim at changing social mindscapes. And those that do so often simply fail. Others gain, lose, and regain discursive strength over time. The 1952 film *High Noon*, initially attacked by many as anti-American, gradually earned a profound educational reputation as a metaphorical warning against silence in the face of tyranny and as a literal case study of the daunting task of leadership. Movies like *The Ox Bow Incident* (1942) and *12 Angry Men* (1957) continue to teach uncomfortable lessons about the critical hazards and crucial demands inherent in any system of criminal justice. The influential power of *12 Angry Men* is evidenced in part by its continued reproduction on screen and stage throughout the world. This includes China, where the context and arguments of *12 Angry Men* were reset into the 2014 film *12 Citizens*.

Readers may be surprised to learn of the numerous efforts made by Chinese filmmakers over the past four decades to challenge prevailing attitudes and policies. In one instance, to be discussed later in this book, a filmmaker's efforts led to a major change Chinese education law. Besides education, our book will present examples of where Chinese cinematic creativity grappled with and called public attention to issues of disaffected youth, rural poverty, and democratic governance. Though such efforts may not always show short-term *success* or *effectiveness* (descriptors with specific meanings to be discussed later in this book), they collectively lend support to the idea that Chinese film producers and viewers alike believe in the potential power of cinematic text to change mindscapes across the People's Republic of China.

China is a nation with a profound history of human drama into which writers, turning fact into fiction, have tapped for centuries. Literature continues to serve Chinese citizens well. Yet as China moves into the 21st century, the drama inherent in the lives of its billion citizens becomes even more profound, more complex, more in need of understanding, and, we suggest, more in need of the kind of storytelling that its independent filmmakers are positioned best to provide. This kind of filmmaking, that upon which this book focuses, represents a combined effort to reach the mind, to educate, and, thus, to lead.

What brought us here?

Building a bridge between leadership theory and Chinese moviemaking seems, admittedly, a long stretch. How we determined a need to build the link is a long story, but one that can be summarized in the form of a short story. Here goes.

An American professor became fascinated with leadership, particularly informal leadership, and its expression in everyday life. For many reasons this seemed to him like a natural pursuit because the word "leadership" had such broad application in the United States and was frequently used to describe the acts of political organizers, fashion designers, football players, and even public school teachers. At a point early in his career, this professor was moved by a paper presentation from Australian scholar Ross Thomas (1998) titled, "As they are Portrayed: Principals in Film." Thomas' analyzed examples of how these school "leaders" were presented in popular films. His examples included *Clockwise* and *Picnic at Hanging Rock*, two films in which the principal's role had little to do with school management literally nothing to do with what most people would call "leadership." This, perhaps, was Thomas' puzzling point; that a principal might "lead" a school only in terms of rank, not because of actions or effect.

Being a film buff, however, the young professor knew of movies with acts, results, and overall themes depicting, if the term had any meaning at all, "leadership." Films such as *To Sir with Love*, in which teacher Mark Thackeray virtually abandons formal curriculum in order to prepare his students for adult life. The film thus became a mainstay of the young professor's course on educational leadership.

Teaching with *To Sir with Love*, however, led to an unavoidable idea – if "educational leadership" could emerge even when teachers fractured the rules of traditional schooling, could it not also emerge in settings entirely outside "the school?" And wasn't such leadership prevalent throughout literature and cinema? One of the young professor's favorite films – *The Man who Shot Liberty Valance* – came to mind. In this classic work from 1962, Jimmy Stewart plays Ransom Stoddard, a greenhorn lawyer who risks his life to teach a group of disconnected townspeople about the value of lawful community. Life, with all its adventure, drama, and challenge, was also a school – as was any book, movie, or other media that could highlight these in the minds of willing students. Another movie thus became part of the professor's course syllabus.

The new and expanded scholarly path seemed clear. But as the professor charted out new definitions of educational leadership, a barricade popped up when of his Chinese students stopped by one day to discuss dissertation ideas. The professor spoke about informal leadership and what a great study it would make were someone to research how it worked in Chinese schools. After several minutes of this, the Chinese student seemed puzzled and said, "I don't know what you mean." Around this same time, the student's confusion was echoed by a group of Taiwan school principals. The professor had asked them, "how do your teachers show *'lingdao'*?"

"What do you mean?" they asked. After probing a bit, one principal replied that her teachers showed leadership by "moving up the ranks" from teacher to department head, to dean, to assistant principal, etc. The professor was perplexed. He'd hit a wall (Schneider, 1979). In Chinese language and culture, it seemed, *lingdao* was tightly connected to formal rank and the downward flow of authority.

As the professor struggled to somehow break through this conceptual wall, another of his Chinese students (now his colleague and main author of this book) picked up on his idea about leadership narratives in popular film. She recommended several Chinese movies depicting themes in which common citizens working toward social change. *Pretty Big Feet* (*Meili de Dajiao*), for example, depicted an aging rural teacher who for decades struggles against harsh local realities to gather popular support for school learning. The documentary *Gao San* (literally "high three" but best translated as *Senior Year*) showed a year in the working life of a teacher in a semi-rural high school who pushes and pulls his sometimes disaffected students through their year of exam hell. These and other movies showed common people expanding their influence – their "authority" – beyond whatever modest formal rank they possessed. Within a Chinese semantic framework, what words or phrases, if not *lingdao* or *lingdaoli*, would convey the social phenomenon presented in these films?

We (yes, your author and coauthor) took another step. If the films presented stories of leadership that led to changes in public thinking, could *lingdao* and *lingdaoli* also encompass the work of Chinese filmmakers – screenwriters, producers, and directors – who individually and collectively create and distribute fresh, meaningful, and socially dynamic messages and insights? Such work – call it cinematic discursive leadership – does not emerge simply by putting "heroes" on the screen. Zhang Yimou's *Not One Less* (*Yige Dou Buneng Shao*) and He Qun's *Country Teachers* (*Fenghuang Qin*) present two young, seemingly hopeless rural schoolteachers who after stumbling through a series of mistakes manage to "pull up their socks" by the end of the movie. Although neither character could be called heroic, both films delivered controversial political messages about Chinese rural education. One, in fact, directly led to a significant change in Chinese education law.

To claim as we do that filmmaking may be an act of *lingdaoli* or that filmmakers may act as *lingdao* might for some seem like banging our heads against the firm wall of culture separating "east and west." Language reflects culture, however, and we see numerous examples of semantic transfer across culture and lexicon. Meanings of words like "love," "marriage," or "education," for instance, gradually evolve over time, despite cultural walls. Over the past two decades, some Chinese scholars in the field of education have raised the idea of "informal leadership" in schools; with the idea gaining greater attention in the process of Chinese education reform. In fact, the very idea that Chinese policy makers saw the need for such reform over the past 20 years is further evidence that cultural walls are more permeable than is typically believed, as many of the new policies reflect similar educational changes in the west. One example of this concerns the recognition that teachers might have the capacity to "lead" their colleagues. The title of "backbone teacher" (*gugan jiaoshi*) is now applied to teachers who show substantial skill in implementing the new classroom practices called for under Chinese educational reform. Although the title represents a formal rank, it also recognizes a form of lateral professional *lingdao*. But could a Chinese teacher – or filmmaker – "show *lingdaoli*" in a larger social context? By answering yes, and by claiming that so, as we bang our heads against the wall arguing that the process and product of filmmaking serve as a form of educational leadership, we also hope to contribute to changes thinking and understanding.

When your authors first launched the idea of filmmaking as educational leadership, some scholars in the field protested by claiming that "educational leadership cannot mean everything!" In return we asked, "who can say?" By this we meant, "who is allowed to say?" No field is owned solely by its fielders. Signifiers like "education" and "leadership," *lingdaoli* and *jiaoyu* travel with us over time, but only in loose configuration with contemporary structure. Ultimately, they represent phenomena unbound from formal schooling or authority. With Chinese cinema as its focus, this book aims to raise awareness of the presence of untethered educational leadership throughout our world.

What we will discuss

The first task – that of outlining some different ideas about educational leadership, formal leadership, *lingdao* and informal leadership – is tackled in Chapter 1 by trying to reveal something of the diversity in the field of leadership among the east and the west. The purpose of this chapter is to show that there are different understandings and images about what education leadership is, what it is for and who is best placed to own it.

At the same time, much of East Asian history and literature, particularly that from China, highlights the non-formal contributions of individual citizens in pursuit of social goals and social change. In other words, "informal leaders" apparently exist within the Chinese social context, but without benefit of being labeled *lingdao*. The range of possibilities presented in Chapter 1, therefore, helps to relate the specific scenario of informal leadership and *lingdao* within a broader context of educational theory and practice. Chapter 2 focuses on this broader context by outlining the major media – Chinese popular films – and examining how they have demonstrated and illustrated the practice of informal leadership within an educational realm. Chapter 2 explores the extent to which these cinematic texts: (1) depict or suggest "Western" understandings of leadership and (2) serve as a discursive medium of social change.

In Chapter 3, based on inductive context analysis of a sample of six Chinese fictional, non-fictional, and documentary films highlighting issues of educational practice and policy, attention is focused on how the potential sociolinguistic impact on the recognition and acceptance of "informal," "bottom up," or "grass roots" leadership within China and other East Asian nations.

Following in Chapter 4, the engagement of Chinese filmmakers in discursive educational leadership is addressed by identifying five emerging themes across a variety of Chinese educational settings where the practice of leadership is presented in terms of the mobilization of collective volition and social change independent of formal rank or position.

Chapter 5 extends the challenge of Chapter 4, outlining other forms of informal discursive leadership compatible with newly evolving media forms popular among Generation Z. The chapter illustrates the power of social media along lines suggested throughout our book.

Note

1 Cardano, G. (1545). *Ars magna or the Rules of Algebra*, Dover (published 1993), ISBN 0-486-67811-3

References

Cardano, G. (1545). *Ars magna, or, the rules of Algebra*, Dover (published 1993), ISBN 0-486-67811-3

Cremin, L. A. (1988). *American education: The metropolitan experience, 1876–1980*. Harper and Row.

Fierz, M. (1983). *Girolamo Cardano, 1501–1576: Physician, natural philosopher, mathematician, astrologer, and interpreter of dreams* (p. 56). Birkhäuser.

Khan, M. S., Khan, I., Qureshi, Q. A., Ismail, H. M., Rauf, H., Latif, A., & Tahir, M. (2015). The styles of leadership: A critical review. *Public Policy and Administration Research, 5*(3), 87–92.

Law, W. W. (2012). Educational leadership and culture in China: Dichotomies between Chinese and Anglo-American leadership traditions? *International Journal of Educational Development, 32*(2), 273–282.

Ma, C., & Shouse, R. C. (2019). Filmmaking as untethered educational leadership: Examples from American and Chinese cinema. *International Journal of Leadership in Education*, 24(6), 760–770.

Schneider, L. A. (1979). *The Dewey experiment in China: Educational reform and political power in the early republic*. By Barry Keenan. Harvard University Press (Harvard East Asian Monographs 81), 1977. xii, 335 pp. Appendixes, Notes, Bibliography, Glossary. Npl. *The Journal of Asian Studies, 38*(2), 336–338.

Shouse, R. C., & Ma, C. (2015). Leadership and creativity in East Asian schools. *Asia Pacific Education Review, 16*, 491–499.

Thomas, A. R. (1998). As they are portrayed: Principals in film. *International Journal of Educational Management, 12*(2), 90–100.

Wang, T., & Gao, S. (2022). Systematic review of research on women and educational leadership in Mainland China, Hong Kong and Taiwan. *Educational Management Administration & Leadership, 0*(0), https://doi.org/10.1177/17411432221142150.

1 Impossible mission I

To distinguish the meaning of "leadership"

We've started out on a slippery endeavor. A "mission impossible." We hope to persuade you that filmmaking and films can be considered acts and artifacts of leadership. We further wish to "lead" you to consider that this idea – not so foreign to Western thinking – has nascent roots in China as well, albeit roots much more complex and contradictory. Ask, for instance, when and how did Chairman Mao Zedong transform from social theorist and local political critic to *lingdao*, and on to *weida de linxiu* (great or historic leader)? And what of Martin Luther King? Our Chinese students also tend to grant him *lingxiu* status, despite the fact he never held any formal position other than that of church minister. Taking a phrase from renown organizational theorist Phillip Selznick (1957), *lingdao* (like leadership) is a slippery concept.

In an everyday world most people can live everyday with slippery understandings of leadership. For instance, it's common to apply the term "leader" whether speaking of a Boy Scout patrol leader or a Microsoft executive. In this sense, however, being called "leader" is not necessarily a recognition of having shown "leadership." People "in charge" will tend to be called "leader" even if they seem incompetent. To make matters more confusing, "incompetent" leaders may be "exercising leadership" even while failing to achieve desired results. In the everyday world we all tend to accept or overlook the puzzling interpretations of leadership and of what it means to "lead."

But in a philosophic or scholarly context, days grow troublesome if conceptual uncertainty permeates thought and literature surrounding such a widely renowned idea as leadership. Uncertainty over the concept flows primarily from its multiple contested and contradictory meanings. For example, in their earliest active years were Martin Luther King and Mao Zedong "leaders" or, perhaps, *ringleaders* (*toumu*)? And what shall we make of the "108 Heroes," the rebels depicted in the classic Chinese novel *Shui Hu Zhuan* who fought for justice against a powerful ruler? How shall we decide when and with whom *lingdao* emerges? One thing we can say with fair certainty is that the word "leadership" serves as a "floating signifier" (Carlson, 2003), a term with uncertain meaning yet useful as a rhetorical device or slogan. It is unlikely, for instance, that a boss who asks you to "show leadership" wants you to stage a rebellion. More likely, the phrase signifies a request for more assistive obedience.

Adding the word "educational" does not clarify matters. For some, educational leadership involves aligning all aspects of teaching and learning with formal organizational authority and policy (Gillies, 2013). For others, the term signifies freedom and diversity with respect to learning or radical new designs for schooling. Social theorist Ivan Illich (1971), for instance, argued for public education to be replaced by local communal learning groups ("convivial education"). In the realm of Western cinema, films like *Lean on Me*, *To Sir with Love*, *School of Rock*, and numerous others honor educational "maverickism" (from "maverick," a word we coin to denote independent or unorthodox tendency). In China, movies like *Country Teachers* and *Not One Less* subtly depict a similar potential for innocent, informal, yet stubborn forms of *jiaoyu lingdao*. Movies like these shape and reshape viewers' thinking about education, and even about society in general. Why, then, is it so difficult to find studies that include literary and cinematic themes within the definition of leadership, educational, or otherwise?

The difficulty stems from several powerful conceptual tendencies, among which are (1) a global linguistic tendency to define leadership as a right restricted to persons holding formal positions of authority; (2) the tendency to frame the concept mainly as an organizational tool; and (3) a tendency to equate "leadership" with "success." That these tendencies overlap in various ways further reflects the slippery nature of leadership. The overlap also may render our discussion a bit looping at times. But it seems fit to begin by describing a matter of key importance to our impossible mission, the philosophy underlying Chinese understandings of *lingdao*.

East Asian perspectives on leadership

The most widely perceived difference in the way leadership is understood in East Asian and Western settings concerns the association of *lingdao* with hierarchical rights of formal rank. In a Chinese school, for example, principals are assumed to lead directors and teachers, directors lead teachers, and teachers lead students. To "lead," in this sense, refers not only to guide and influence but also to act as superordinate. Subordinates might influence their bosses, but they do not "lead" them. This meaning persists in Mandarin despite numerous historic and everyday examples of subordinate persons, groups, or officials attempting to exercise what in the United States would be called "upward leadership" or "dynamic subordinancy" (Lee & Ip, 2023). In China, however, upward influence would occur more gradually or indirectly and would rarely be called *lingdao*.

China's formalistic top-down understandings of leadership have been shaped by five fundamental guiding philosophies as applied by numerous emperors throughout the nation's history – Taoism, Confucianism, Mohism, Legalism, and Militarism (Chen, 1995; Law, 2012; Sia, 1997; Wang, 2007; Wang & Chee, 2011; Wong, 2001). Together, these philosophies have produced subtle, complex, and powerful norms of meaning. Prevalent among these are collectivism, power distance, hierarchy, and harmony. Chinese collectivism reveals itself in people's willingness to accept the needs and goals of the larger groups to which they belong; to coordinate or suspend their own needs and goals with respect to the larger groups. Power distance is about how people perceive and compare their own social efficacy to that of greater legal, administrative, or political authority; to put simply, do people believe they can "fight city hall"? Hierarchical understandings are evident in many areas of Chinese life. Fathers tend to be deeply respected, as are older brothers by their younger siblings. Such cultural dispositions remain strong despite the democratization trends across East Asia in recent decades.

In particular, social status remains a highly salient indicator of individual value and character. Intellectual work, for example, is ascribed higher status than most forms of physical labor, a disposition likely related to an over 2000-year-old system of meritocratic exams and to a generalized belief that education was indicative of high moral character.

In addition to these dispositions, the importance placed by East Asian societies upon maintaining "social harmony" cannot be underestimated. In general, conflict is to be avoided or, at least, occur subtly or outside public view. Consideration is given to preserving "face" or dignity for oneself and those with whom one interacts. The value placed upon social harmony fundamentally shapes "leadership concepts and practices, expectations and responses" (Shah, 2006, p. 365). Taken together, these dispositions facilitate and reinforce the idea of hierarchy in social and organizational settings. As individuals move upward in terms of social or organizational rank, they acquire well-understood rights of authority. Such understandings change the idea of a leader from "someone who does something" to "someone who is something" (Shouse & Lin, 2010, p. 24).

Thus, while Western views tend to link leadership to change via persuasion, Eastern views tend to associate it with stability via experience, wisdom, and "obedience." Change, of course, still occurs in Eastern societies, but more slowly, more cautiously, and from the top down.

Theoretically and empirically, however, the problem with this traditional Chinese narrative is that although Western ideas of diffuse egalitarian leadership may lack legitimacy in Chinese settings, we nevertheless see them in action. We've previously asked, for instance, whether examples in China of upward influence – or even historically successful acts disobedience or insurrection – could be considered acts of leadership. The question can also be asked about the "non-formal" efforts of Chinese citizens, including writers and filmmakers, to engage in social persuasion.

Leadership as non-formal human endeavor

Alongside the somewhat restrictive semantic norms surrounding the idea of *lingdao*, one also sees restrictions, less rigid perhaps, on the Western meaning of *leadership*. Though loose usage of the word "leader" is common in the West, restrictions tighten as one moves more deeply into realms of organization theory, education, or philosophy. In such contexts, naturalistic understandings of leadership are hindered by two tightly connected discursive problems. One involves the way in which leadership studies become nested within organizational contexts, typically industry, politics, or education. The idea of leadership thus falls victim to instrumentalism, situated as a tool for attaining formal goals. For example, your authors recall a conversation with the dean of a major American college of education on the topic of "teacher leadership." One of us mentioned that this might take the form of teachers' "constructive disobedience" regarding administrative control over classroom practice. The dean responded with silent bemusement. His teacher leadership degree program launched the following year, with a focus on "school improvement," at the time, a widely used euphemism for "increasing test scores."

This leads to the related problem. Leadership literature and educational leadership literature, in particular, often start with the question of what it means to "lead effectively." The word "effectiveness" then pulls the discussion back to organizational instrumentalism, formality, hierarchy, and successful outcome. Effective leaders attain their goals; weak leaders do not. Is this not like equating "love" with marriage or "creativity" with acclaim? Love, creativity, and leadership exist, we suggest, even when their efforts appear to fail. (We expand on this – with respect to leadership – later in this chapter.)

Return now to the key challenge of our impossible mission. A ubiquitous natural phenomenon exists – a human desire to change the minds and actions of others within a given social unit or arena. Yet nearly universally, linguistic designations of "leadership" only partially align with the natural phenomenon. Across cultures and languages words comparable to "leadership" or *lingdao* almost invariably refer to acts or positions within formal hierarchical contexts.

At first glance, this challenge seems to be one of semantics, one of focusing on what a particular word means. The problem, however, is actually *onomasiological*, a question of whether or how an observed phenomenon or concept is represented in words. *Lingdaoli*, for example, has generalized meaning that includes some of, but not all, the meaning associated with the word "leadership." You may thus "argue semantics" over the meaning of either word with your Chinese or American friend. Can teachers "lead" their schools? Can filmmakers exercise *lingdao* outside their formal organizational role? Regardless of how one answers, the natural human phenomenon of leading *exists and has existed long prior to* the establishment of formal organization.

Language *normatively* designates who may be called *leader*. But norms, language, and semantics nonetheless remain socially negotiated over time.

This, of course, is our impossible mission. Our argument aims to untether the meaning of educational leadership and *jiaoyu lingdao* from formal organizational hierarchy, and to launch the idea that this new meaning can encompass the work and products of filmmakers.

The idea that *lingdao* and *leadership* can denote *untethered* (Ma & Shouse, 2019) efforts of filmmakers (or artists, writers, etc.) to engage in social influence rests on the lines of 20th-century thought. This isn't to say that leadership thought began in the 1900s. Writings by men like Lao Tsu and Machiavelli certainly deal with questions of how to effectively move large groups of people toward desired goals. But such works deal primarily with the acquisition and maintenance of power, essentially through any means necessary. Such visions conflate "leadership" with "power," and the truth is that the two concepts are closely related. Though successful leadership serves as a source of power, it is soft power. Coercive acts may at some point assist a leader. But only in the barest sense can a tyrant be called a leader, though tomorrow's tyrant might certainly employ leadership today. Most political tyrants, in fact, rely on leadership in the earliest stage of their careers.

What distinguishes 20th-century thought, however, is a recognition that leadership represents the potential to *mobilize volition*, to generate within social units a willingness (based not primarily on fear or coercion) to suspend personal judgment in favor of that of another person or group. Members and potential group members gradually and voluntarily come to accept ideas or actions previously not considered to be necessary or valuable.

A good example of this is found in the 1957 film, *12 Angry Men*, a work that has over the years been translated and reconfigured across various languages and countries (including China). In the American version, a man known only as Juror 8 stands alone against 11 other jurors. Though Juror 8 has no special standing (he is not the jury foreman), he gradually persuades the others to find a young murder suspect not guilty. What characteristic has Juror 8 shown? Does the film itself caution and remind viewers about the edgy balance between criminal justice and individual rights? Does not the process of making the movie constitute an effort to change viewers' thinking? Does the film succeed in this regard? We suggest that the entire entity of *12 Angry Men*, from its original teleplay through its global adaptations, represents a vector of educational leadership across time and space, whose influence or success is never quite certain yet at the same time never absent.

Leadership implies action, not result

But what if *12 Angry Men* had ended with most of the other jurors voting to convict along with a final shot of Juror 8's frustrated and disheartened face?

Because American criminal jurisprudence requires unanimous verdicts, the result would have been a mistrial; audiences would have to ponder what might happen in a new trial. In this event would the film have less persuasive impact? In fact, an earlier American film, *The Ox Bow Incident*, sharply raises this question. Here, a small group of cowboys (including one also performed by the actor who played Juror 8) try to stop a larger posse from lynching three alleged cattle thieves. Based on a novel, the film challenges audiences in the same way as *12 Angry Men*. We don't want to give away the ending but suffice to say *The Ox Bow Incident* also challenges us to abandon the idea that leadership must be successful to be called *leadership*.

In fact, most attempts at leadership are either unrecognized or unsuccessful. Noting this reality in the mid-20th century, organizational theorist J.K. Hemphill posited three categories of leadership. First, he noted, leadership is often *attempted* but with little notice or influence. *Successful* leadership, he argued, comprises acts resulting in partial influence, but little substantial result. Finally, according to Hemphill, *effective* leadership is that which changes minds and attains desired results. Hemphill presents his idea as a triangle divided horizontally into three parts so as to indicate that the greatest and least prevalent forms of leadership are, respectively, attempted and effective.

Hemphill's perspective allows leadership acts to be perceived in their early formative stages and as they evolve or fail over time. Acts and works intended to influence, whether social, political, or artistic often have little impact when launched. Books, films, or vision statements can lie dormant for years or decades before becoming influential. Also note how examples of attempted or partially successful leadership are often highlighted in literature and film. The paths of history may be lined with the remnants of failed leadership, yet a historic noble failure may eventually help launch a powerful successful campaign.

Leadership as vector

Considering the ubiquitous and evolving nature of leadership, another good way to think about it is to imagine it as a force with direction and magnitude – a *vector* of social influence across time and social context (Shouse & Ma, 2015). A comprehensive example of this is found in the global wave of "school reform" that emerged toward the late 20th century. What first triggered this wave is unclear, though by the 1990s several East Asian scholars, some of who had studied in the United States, began calling for curricular and instructional change in their own nations' school systems. One of the earliest of these was Nobel Prize winning chemist Yuan T. Lee, whose calls for "creative" and "whole child" schooling helped launch a major school reform effort in China-Taiwan. Similar reform efforts gradually spread across China's mainland, often in the form of what became known as *suzhi jiaoyu* ("quality education"). Over a roughly similar period, perhaps triggered by the alleged successes of traditional East-Asian education, American education policy leaders began to advocate more "high-stakes" testing, particularly in math and science, along with commensurate cutbacks in areas like art, music, and even recess. Though propelled by "leaders" on both sides of the Pacific Ocean, neither movement achieved substantial success. Though many factors impeded the proposed reforms (Dello-Iacovo, 2009; Lin, 2011), overall failure likely resulted from persons and groups formally and informally championing different educational visions. Think of this as an emerging field of conflicting leadership vectors, which will be illustrated elaborately later in Chapter 2.

Although this imagery of formal and informal leadership vectors conflicting and interacting across time and space may be more compatible with Western leadership theory, it is seen nearly universally, especially during times of rising social uncertainty and expectation. In China, educational reform represents one clear example of a leadership vector field. Yet other less obvious playing fields exist in China, for example, that which is occupied by artists, writers, and filmmakers. In this arena, attention turns to the idea of discursive leadership and "ghost" leadership.

Discursive leadership, ghost leadership, and cinematic leadership

The "everyday leadership" of which we speak lurks and emerges in the form of words and symbols, in speech, text, and visual media. The term "discursive leadership" is often used to describe this phenomenon (Fairhurst, 2007), and the term "ghost leadership" has been applied when persuasive meaning is expressed by long-passed storytellers, writers, and the characters they've used to express such meaning (Auvinen, 2012). The key idea here refers to the ways in which *discourse* – words, texts, and narratives become powerful tools for shaping social meaning.

Also useful here is Michel Foucault's concept of *Discourse* (signified as a proper noun) referring to gradually constructed and interacting networks of thought and structure that work to reify meaning – to create "regimes of truth" (Foucault, 1980). Consider, for instance, how the early idea of mass schooling led to a belief in the necessity for "school administration." Over time, this belief spread to promote normative conceptions of the organizational structure and type of "educational leadership" necessary to effectively administer mass schooling. In turn emerged a delineated *discipline* or *field* of leadership with an eye fixed on the actions of school administrators and policy makers. By laying out the topics and knowledge considered appropriate or necessary for study, the *field* contributes to a self-replicating apparatus (Foucault's *dispositif*) that authoritatively controls the meanings we attach to "school," "teaching," "education," and "leadership."

Another example of discourse in education is the gradual construction of the STEM concept, which imposes a heavy responsibility on public schools to emphasize learning in science, technology, engineering, and math. These have always been part of American schooling, especially since the late 1950s. But the past 30 years have seen a trend by which schools were expected to treat student test scores in these subjects as prima facie evidence of organizational effectiveness. Other studies indicate how this "truth" resulted from a chain of observations and occurrences dating back to the so-called Coleman Report of the mid-1960s. The first large-scale statistical analysis of American public school effectiveness examined how individual, organizational, and family factors influenced achievement test scores in English, history, math, and science.

As the study advanced, its authors reasoned math scores to be the most valid and robust indicators of achievement, not because of greater importance, but because math knowledge was least influenced by students' experiences outside of school. Mathematical knowledge was also easy to test in standardized fashion and later school studies adopted it as a primary measure of student learning and school quality. By the 1980s, Americans were being frequently alerted to an apparent gap in math achievement scores between students in Asia and the United States. Warnings were issued with warlike imagery (e.g., "A Nation at Risk"). Advances in the power and availability of personal computing promoted increased awareness of the various "gaps" in math learning across nations, races, and genders. By the 1990s, STEM became a key driver for President Bush's "No Child Left Behind" initiative as well as for increased calls for greater centralization of American school curriculum (e.g., "Race to the Top"). As the STEM narrative came to predominate official thinking on American schools, "secondary" areas such as art, music, and even elementary school recess were cut back to provide more time and resources for the new STEM testing regime. At least one major American scholar asserted that school "leadership" could not be considered "legitimate" unless it focused on raising student test scores (Ihrig et al., 2018; Khalil & Kier, 2021; Peus et al., 2013).

As is often the case throughout American educational history, brakes have been recently applied to the STEM bandwagon. Attention shifted to the value of creativity and a perceived recognition that this was an area of strength among American students. Parents, alarmed at the amount of testing and test prep imposed upon their children began to revolt, in many cases keeping their children home from school during testing days. Instead of raising greater public alarm, the 2008 documentary film *Two Million Minutes* (which critically clashed the free and loosely structured US high school experience with the far more rigorous and constricted offerings of India and China) prompted the release of *Race to Nowhere*, a 2009 documentary film highlighting the alleged negative impact of school intensification.

Over time, it thus becomes quite apparent how the meanings we attach to matters like education, justice, and even to words themselves are deeply influenced through the creation of narratives and discourse. Through storytelling and other forms of rhetoric, "leaders" are in fact said to be "managers of meaning" (Smirich & Morgan, 1982). But as should be clear by now, managing meaning is an endeavor open not only to appointed captains but also to anyone with the will and capacity to place a hand on the wheel. "Meaning," it appears, isn't managed. Rather, it is negotiated and renegotiated with new ideas, new arguments, and new stories. And since the moment cinematic text came into being, its creators have been part of the conversation.

The launching of words, symbols, stories, and actions are all part of vast conversation from which leadership arises. Ideas flow, people view them as useful or wise, and thought and behavior are changed (Robinson, 2001). By changing and mobilizing thought, skillfully constructed cinematic texts launch vectors of informal leadership (Shouse, 2005; Thomas, 1998; Wang, 2009).

Can non-formal leadership thought apply to China?

In the capacity to control the creation and distribution of cinematic texts lies the potential capacity to construct social narratives. Wang (2009), for example, has described the shift occurring within post-revolutionary Chinese cinema from a place highlighting movie "stars" to one that espoused "revolutionary culture." Chinese popular films of the 1950s became a useful field from which to launch attacks or endorsements of various ideological beliefs and positions.

Although the ability to produce and control the content and distribution of cinematic texts was early on mainly the province of powerful and wealthy interests (e.g., governments and large studios), this has changed over time even in China. Since the nation's "opening up" in the late 1970s, Chinese film researchers (Mao, 2011; Zhou, 2009) have noted a cinematic shift from presenting formal normative depictions of appropriate moral or civic lessons to offering more problematized perspectives. Although filmmakers can risk losing formal government authorization for their work, it has become more difficult today for governments to block the distribution of these works outside their national boundaries. For example, movies like *Please Vote for Me* and *Balzac and the Little Chinese Seamstress* (both filmed in China) were globally acclaimed despite restricted distribution in China. The widening availability of film as a discursive resource has greatly expanded the power of filmmakers to reshape social narratives, mobilize public volition, and, hence, to lead.

References

Auvinen, T. (2012). The ghost leader: An empirical study on narrative leadership. *EJBO: Electronic Journal of Business Ethics and Organizational Studies, 17*(1), 4–15.

Carlson, D. (2003). Troubling heroes: Of Rosa Parks, multicultural education, and critical pedagogy. *Cultural Studies? Critical Methodologies, 3*(1), 44–61.

Chen, M. (1995). *Asian management systems: Chinese, Japanese and Korean styles of business*. Routledge.

Dello-Iacovo, B. (2009). Curriculum reform and 'quality education' in China: An overview. *International Journal of Educational Development, 29*(3), 241–249.

Fairhurst, G. (2007). *Discursive leadership: In conversation with leadership psychology*. Sage.

Foucault, M. (1980). *On the government of the living: Lectures at the Collège de France, 1979–1980*. Springer.

Gillies, D. (2013). *Educational leadership and Michel Foucault*. Routledge.

Ihrig, L. M., Lane, E., Mahatmya, D., & Assouline, S. G. (2018). STEM excellence and leadership program: Increasing the level of STEM challenge and engagement for high-achieving students in economically disadvantaged rural communities. *Journal for the Education of the Gifted, 41*(1), 24–42.

Illich, I. (1971). *Deschooling society*. Routledge.

Khalil, D., & Kier, M. (2021). Equity-centered design thinking in STEM instructional leadership. *Journal of Cases in Educational Leadership, 24*(1), 69–85.

Law, W. W. (2012). Educational leadership and culture in China: Dichotomies between Chinese and Anglo-American leadership traditions? *International Journal of Educational Development, 32*(2), 273–282.

Lee, D. H. L., & Ip, N. K. K. (2023). The influence of professional learning communities on informal teacher leadership in a Chinese hierarchical school context. *Educational Management Administration & Leadership, 51*(2), 324–344.

Lin, Y. (2011). Turning rurality into modernity: Suzhi education in a suburban public school of migrant children in Xiamen. *The China Quarterly, 206*, 313–330.

Mao, Y. (2011). Educational discourse in film: The history of Chinese educational documentaries. *Front Education China, 6*(4), 620–638. doi:10.1007/s11516-011-0148-9

Ma, C., & Shouse, R. C. (2019). Filmmaking as untethered educational leadership: Examples from American and Chinese cinema. *International Journal of Leadership in Education, 24*(6), 760–770.

Peus, C., Braun, S., & Frey, D. (2013). Situation-based measurement of the full range of leadership model—Development and validation of a situational judgment test. *The Leadership Quarterly, 24*(5), 777–795.

Robinson, V. M. (2001). Embedding leadership in task performance. In Kam-cheung Wong and Colen W. Evers (Ed.), *Leadership for Quality Schooling: International Perspectives* (pp. 90–102). Routledge.

Selznick, P. (1957). *Leadership in administration: A sociological interpretation*. Harper & Row.

Shah, S. (2006). Educational leadership: An Islamic perspective. *British Educational Research Journal, 32*(3), 363–385.

Shouse, R. C. (2005). Taking Lulu seriously: What we can learn from "To Sir with Love". *Journal of Educational Administration, 43*(4), 357–367.

Shouse, R. C., & Lin, K. P. (2010). *Principal leadership in Taiwan schools*. Rowman & Littlefield Publishers.

Shouse, R. C., & Ma, C. (2015). Leadership and creativity in East Asian schools. *Asia Pacific Education Review, 16*, 491–499.

Sia, A. (1997). *The Chinese art of leadership*. Asiapac.

Smircich, L., & Morgan, G. (1982). Leadership: The management of meaning. *The Journal of Applied Behavioral Science, 18*(3), 257–273.

Thomas, A. R. (1998). As they are portrayed: Principals in film. *International Journal of Educational Management, 12*(2), 90–100.
Wang, T. (2007). Understanding Chinese educational leaders' conceptions in an international education context. *International Journal of Leadership in Education, 10*(1), 71–88. doi:10.1080/13603120500445275
Wang, X. (2009). Three studies in recent trends of modern Chinese literature and culture. *China Perspectives*, (2009/4), 118–126.
Wang, B. X., & Chee, H. (2011). *Chinese leadership*. Palgrave Macmillan.
Wong, K. C. (2001). Chinese culture and leadership. *International Journal of Leadership in Education, 4*(4), 309–319. doi:10.1080/13603120110077990
Zhou, X. L. (2009). Screening education: Schools on film in the People's Republic of China. *Sungkyun Journal of East Asian Studies, 9*(2), 213–230.

2 Impossible mission II
To depict the film as discursive leadership

Throughout history and across cultures, education has advanced through the creative organization and presentation of narrative, symbol, sound, and image. Disconnected from formal authority or institution, storytelling, art, music, and literature have shown a marked ability to teach, inspire, and "change the minds" of people and groups. For more than a century and with varying success, filmmakers have intersected these textual avenues into units of meaning. When successful, their works move beyond entertainment to become powerful agents for civic education and social change. Over 30 years ago, in fact, educational historian Lawrence Cremin (1988) wrote of the "immense power" of movies to reshape the beliefs, attitudes, and even the language of viewers.

This capacity and process seem consistent with the concept of "leadership" as understood in many semantic contexts, particularly when advanced by individuals or groups. In many sociolinguistic contexts, however, the "leadership" concept and its semantic representations tend to be reserved for persons or groups with formal status; e.g., a president, CEO, or school principal. In China, for example, the Mandarin word *lingdao* rarely applied to efforts of social influence outside a chain of command. More specifically, the concept of leadership – and the corresponding Mandarin word, *lingdao, lingdaoli* (Wehmeier, 2004) – seemed to carry different connotations on each side of the Pacific Ocean (Hong & Engeström, 2004; Law, 2012). Given China's rich history and literature with respect to individual acts of heroism and patriotism, this linguistic gap seems rather odd.

Thus, we arrive at the questions which drive our study. First, what is a "leader?" From an Eastern point of view, if a leader is simply "the person in charge," then why do we need other words corresponding with "leader" such as "authority," "manager," or simply "the boss?" And what about the word "leadership?" Does it merely refer to the legitimate acts of people "in charge?" Or can leadership be distinguished from these various related concepts? If so, would that imply that "leadership" isn't restricted to acts of those in charge, but could be evidenced across a broader range of human interaction? Could common understandings of this widely appreciated concept be achieved? Would it be possible to find an interesting, intuitive, and easy-to-understand

DOI: 10.4324/9781032723778-3

way to comprehend and unite the essence of educational leadership across cultural boundaries? Can cinematic form be the special way to express socio-educational leadership?

Basic assumptions of leader, leadership, East and West

Nearly everywhere, it seems, people expect "leadership," though not always in the same form or with the same function. For some, leadership involves living or working within various structures of organized authority as represented by persons known as "leader." These structures and persons may be perceived as weak or strong; e.g., mayor, boss, school principal, scoutmaster, or head of a local neighborhood group. It's not that we expect to be literally "led" anywhere. We simply assume that someone will be "in charge" and that this person shall be formally or informally known as "leader." Often, however, people do expect leadership to involve the transition of ideas or action in ways beneficial to themselves or others. Yet those who claim "we need leadership" may mean that whatever transition occurs should impact not themselves, but other individuals or groups. In this sense, "strong leadership" is attributed to the person or persons who help us "have our own way." Odder yet, the word "leader" is sometimes applied to tyrants whose "leadership" involves physical threat or intimidation.

"Leadership," at least in its Western sense, is a "slippery concept" (Katz & Kahn, 1966; Selznick, 1957), understood and symbolized in various ways. The same may be said for other human concepts (consider "love" or "creativity"). But for "leadership" to be seriously studied, as it is around the world and across numerous fields of social science, deserves a distinctive definition. This requires several steps. For example, one must recognize that the central ideas of leadership and *lingdao* are substantially distinct from other related ideas such as "management," "authority," or "power." At its core, leadership involves a flow of influence intended to result in voluntary change by persons or groups. Management (*guanli*, in Mandarin), at its core, represents a focus on maintaining reliability across a complex system. It's true, of course, that managers may sometimes need to "lead," and that "leaders" may sometimes need to "manage." But it is also true that management almost always involves formal position of authority.

But "authority" is not simply about holding hierarchical position. Police officers, school principals, and office managers are often referred to as "authorities." At its core, however, authority is about voluntary compliance. People grant authority to others (Barnard, 1938). They allow it to exist and, sometimes, allow it to grow beyond the boundaries of formal position. This voluntary granting of authority is another key distinguisher of "leadership." We recognize "leadership" when we see people changing prior patterns of belief or action in response to the influence of those attempting to lead. As willingness replaces resistance, leadership becomes a form of "power." But again, those possessing power – like those possessing authority – are not necessarily accomplishing "leadership." Though assigned positions of authority and generally referred to as leaders, school principals may lack the power to compel broad pedagogical changes within their school. Principals may apply formal sanctions to enforce teacher compliance but, doing so may, over time, damage their authority and leadership capacity.

Despite such distinctions, "leadership" remains a nebulous concept and, often, a rhetorical tool. Some claim it to be little more than empty or "floating" signifier used to signify actions we approve or belittle those we do not (Carlson, 2003). Past successes or defeats of major proportion, for instance, are often viewed as resulting from great or inadequate leadership. Alternatively, a supervisor's suggestion to "show more leadership" may represent a demand for greater compliance or longer work hours from an employee (McGurk, 2009). Floating signifiers in a sense represent the nebulization of a concept – a reasonably solid idea becomes vaguely applied wherever it seems useful. This happens frequently in everyday speech. At the same time, nebulization may enable a word-concept to become a powerful rhetorical tool, commandeered to expand and empower a particular discourse of social control; e.g., a particular (often contestable) agenda of educational practice, policy, or reform is claimed to represent "educational leadership" (Bredeson & Kose, 2007).

It's true that social phenomena will be observed and understood in different ways, multiple overlapping concepts will emerge, and the resulting descriptions of these concepts will also overlap. Situations involving social influence and change, for instance, are commonly (though not solely) described in terms "leadership," "authority," and "power" or their Mandarin counterparts *lingdao, quanwei, and quanli*. Whether understood in English or Mandarin, a Venn diagram relating these words and their underlying ideas would show three distinct non-concentric circles, as shown in Figure 2.1.

That is, in both China and the United States, it is recognized that none of their meanings are considered contained within nor identical to the meaning of another. Studies of "leadership" in both countries often begin with this understanding but then often blur the distinctions, shifting focus to the use of leadership by persons in formal positions of authority. This is particularly true across the field known as "educational leadership" (Spillane, 2004). Given that countless books and articles focus on the meaning and use of "leadership" (especially "educational leadership"), it seems crucial to distinguish its meaning from these other-related concepts. One thus asks, what is the essence of leadership? What does it denote that related concepts do not?

Having already hinted at what we believe to be the core meaning of "leadership" and *lingdao*, further clarification is needed, particularly in terms of what they are not. In both China and the United States, scholarly

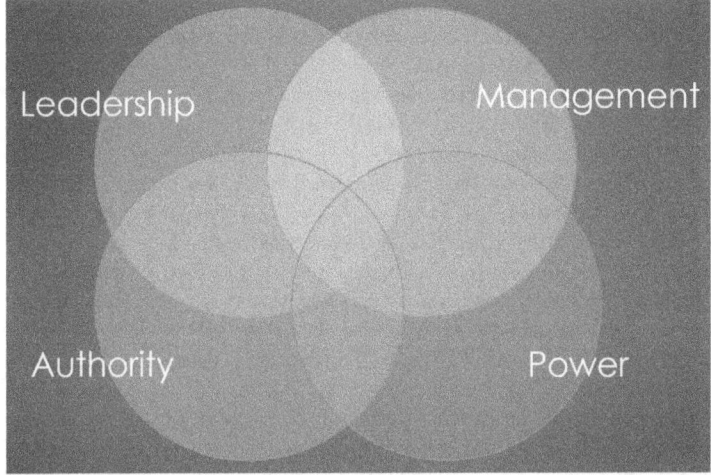

Figure 2.1 Relationship between Leadership, Management, Authority and Power

understandings distinguish the leadership concept from management, power, or authority in that

> ...leadership represents the changing of minds and the mobilization of collective volition. Leadership is the process by which individuals and communities gradually and voluntarily come to accept ideas or products they had previously believed were unnecessary, unwise, or irrelevant.
> (Shouse & Ma, 2015)

As we mentioned earlier, leadership is said to be a "slippery phenomenon" (Selznick, 1957). Perhaps this is because even in the West it is imbued with multiple and often contradictory meanings, even within scholarly literature. On top of that, it is a concept that is very familiar to average people, yet one that they may find very difficult to define. For some, the word serves purposes of a "floating signifier" (Carlson, 2003), a term with contested meaning often used as a rhetorical or political device (Shouse & Lin, 2010). Adding the word "educational" to "leadership" does not clarify matters. For some, "educational leadership" involves administrators, policies, change, and even obedience to higher authority. For others, it may signify an opening for radical new designs for schooling and learning. The key point, perhaps, is that "leadership," even in its "western sense," has often become entangled with and mistaken for the specific goals sought by those calling for "leadership."

In addition, "leadership" is often lumped together with other related concepts such as "authority," "power," and "management." For over a century, scholars have sought to distinguish these terms, and yet their differences – and their connections – often remain obscure. Given that countless books and articles focus on the meaning and use of "leadership" (especially "educational leadership"), it seems crucial to distinguish its meaning from these other related concepts. One thus asks, what is the essence of leadership? What does it denote that related concepts do not?

Based on ideas presented in prior studies (see, for example, Barnard, 1938; Haller & Strike, 1986; Hoy & Miskel, 2001; Shouse & Lin, 2010), it is suggested here that leadership involves actions aimed at mobilizing volition toward the acceptance of individual, social, or political change. Change is achieved primarily through non-coercive persuasion, where individuals or groups gradually accept ideas or actions they previously had not considered to be necessary or valuable. Chester Barnard (1938) described leadership as a form of authority that could emerge from individuals regardless of their formal position. In similar terms, leadership represents the expansion of what Barnard (1938) called the "zone of indifference" and what Herbert (1957) later termed the "zone of acceptance," an imaginary space wherein lies the various directives or suggestions for which potential followers will suspend their own judgment in favor of that of the potential leader. As the zone expands, authority grows allowing leadership to occur. In other words, leadership aims at mobilizing volition for purposes of goal attainment or change. "Educational leadership" can thus be broadly viewed at such efforts that are related to processes of organized and/or deliberate learning.

At the same time, no objective justification exists to assume any congruence between leadership exercised within organizations and formal organizational goals. As Gary Yukl (1998) suggests, leadership is a process in which all members of an organization may influence and reshape its goals, processes, outcomes, and power relationships. Or, as stated by Hoy and Miskel (2001, p. 394), "leadership is comprised of both rational and emotional elements with no assumptions about the purpose or outcome of the influential efforts."

It is also important to note, that "leadership" is not defined by success. Hemphill (1949) emphasizes, in contrast, three categories of leadership; attempted (acts resulting in little or no influence); successful (resulting in some influence); and effective (resulting in change or goal attainment). Hemphill's perspective allows leadership acts to be perceived in their early formative stages and helps avoid the tendency to apply the word "leader" primarily as an indicator of past success. In many cases, acts of leadership are neither effective nor highly successful at the time they occur. Such forms of attempted leadership, in fact, often serve as the basis for literature and film.

Thus, another good way to think about leadership as a phenomenon is to think of it as a vector of social influence with widely diverse potential for direction and magnitude within social units. While such descriptions may seem more compatible with Western leadership theory, it is important to remember that such vectors are evident in nearly every social unit, especially at times when uncertainty and expectation are on the rise. This description is applicable to school systems throughout East Asia and China in particular.

East Asian Perspectives

According to a range of empirical and theoretical studies, the most widely perceived difference in the way leadership is understood in East Asian and Western settings relates to its association with formal positions of authority. In East Asian political and organizational settings, the possession or exercise of leadership or *lingdao* is tightly linked to formal rank and is understood to flow from "authority" to "subordinate" (Shouse & Lin, 2010). In a Chinese school, for example, the norm of understanding tends to be that principals "lead" directors and teachers, directors lead teachers, and teachers lead students.

As previously discussed, in Western settings, the above description is just one of several diverse understandings of what it means to lead. As Hoy and Miskel (2001) suggest, leadership is understood as a phenomenon that can arise from any point within an organization and that can flow in any direction. Leadership may work to support or, in some situations, to block or change formal organizational goals and procedures (Shouse & Lin, 2010). This diffuse and somewhat egalitarian interpretation of leadership is likely rooted in traditional Western philosophies stressing equality, freedom, and the rights of individuals.

In contrast, the meaning of leadership In China has been shaped by five fundamental guiding philosophies as applied by numerous emperors throughout the nation's history – Taoism, Confucianism, Mohism, Legalism, and Militarism (Chen, 1995; Law, 2012; Sia, 1997; Wang, 2007; Wang & Chee, 2011; Wong, 2001). Together, these philosophies have produced themes of meaning that are often complex, subtle, and contrasting with Western perspectives. Prevalent among these themes in today's China (and throughout East Asia) are collectivism, power distance, and a pronounced social status structure (Bush & Qiang, 2002; Hofstede et al., 1991; Shouse & Lin, 2010). Collectivism refers to the willingness of individuals to identify with the needs and goals of the larger groups to which they belong; more specifically, to coordinate or suspend their own needs and goals with respect to the larger groups. Power distance refers to how remote citizens perceive themselves from legal, administrative, or political authority. To put it in terms of an old American saying, power distance represents the degree to which citizens believe they can "fight city hall." Such cultural dispositions remain strong despite the democratization trends occurring throughout East Asia over past decades. In particular, social status remains a highly salient indicator of individual value and character. Intellectual work, for example, is ascribed higher status than most forms of physical labor, a disposition likely related to an over 2000-year-old system of meritocratic exams and to a generalized belief that education was indicative of high moral character.

In addition to these dispositions, the importance placed by East Asian societies upon maintaining "social harmony" should not be underestimated. In general, conflict is something to be avoided or, at least, to occur subtly or outside of public view. Consideration is given to preserving "face" or dignity for oneself and those with whom one interacts. The value placed upon social harmony fundamentally shapes "leadership concepts and practices, expectations and responses" (Shah, 2006, p. 365). Taken together, these dispositions facilitate and reinforce the idea of hierarchy in social and organizational settings. As individuals move upward in terms of social or organizational rank, they acquire rights of authority that are generally well-understood by others. As Shouse and Lin (2010, p. 24) suggest, such understanding changes the idea of leader from "someone who does something" to "someone who is something."

It thus seems fair to suggest that while Western views tend to link leadership to change via persuasion, Eastern views tend to associate it with stability via experience, wisdom, and "obedience." Change, of course, still occurs in Eastern societies, but it tends to occur slowly, carefully, and from the top down.

From both theoretical and empirical perspectives, however, the problem with this narrative is that although Western ideas of diffuse egalitarian leadership may lack legitimacy in Eastern settings, one nevertheless sees them in action. For example, when he first began to mobilize followers and launch a revolution against established formal authority, was Mao Zedong engaged in Chinese "leadership?" The same question can be asked with regard to other Chinese citizens, including writers and filmmakers who engage in public acts of social persuasion. The questions raised here flow from the cultural and conceptual tensions that we hope to examine more fully throughout this study.

The film as discursive leadership

The term "discursive leadership" (Fairhurst, 2007) circumscribes a set of ideas related to the use of words, texts, and narratives as tools for the shaping of social meaning. In this regard, various scholars (Ross Thomas, 1998; Shouse, 2005, 2009; Wang, 2009) have highlighted how cinematic texts operate in two important ways. First, the stories presented within the film provide opportunities for understanding particular social problems and, in some instances, also suggest ways to address them. Second, those who control the creation and distribution of cinematic texts acquire the potential capacity to construct larger social narratives. Wang (2009), for example, describes the shift occurring within post-revolutionary Chinese cinema "from star to revolutionary culture," as popular film became a useful field of play for government officials and party members to advance or attack particular ideological understandings.

Once mainly the province of powerful and wealthy interests (e.g., governments and large studios), over time and globally, the ability to produce and control the content and distribution of cinematic texts has expanded. Examples of this trend are described in Mao's (2011) study of Chinese documentary films and Zhou's (2009) study of Chinese "schools on film." Both studies describe a gradual change from films presenting formal "normative" depictions of life and education (e.g., appropriate moral or civic lessons) to films offering more problematized perspectives. Despite the fact that filmmakers often risk losing formal government authorization for their work, it has become far more difficult today for governments to block distribution of these works outside their national boundaries. For example, movies like *Please Vote for Me* (see Chapter 4) and *Balzac and the Little Chinese Seamstress* were both filmed in China and highly regarded outside of China despite having their distribution blocked within China. The widening availability of film as a discursive resource has greatly expanded the power of filmmakers to reshape social narratives, mobilize public volition, and, hence, to lead.

To summarize, we offer Robinson's (2001, p. 93) definition of leadership, which seems congruent with the idea of mobilized volition:

> …Leadership is exercised when ideas expressed in talk or action are recognized by others as capable of progressing tasks or problems which are important to them.

In terms of the present study, the important point here is that skillful cinematic texts work as vectors of social influence, mobilization, and leadership. They constitute informal vectors of leadership to the extent their creation and distribution lie beyond authorized position or systematic government control.

Leadership, education, and social learning

Up to now, our book has drawn several inferences and conclusions that require further discussion. Of note here are the following: (1) that leadership (or *lingdao*) is a social phenomenon that can occur informally within and outside of formal organizations and (2) that "learning," "education," and "educational leadership" are closely linked phenomena that can occur formally or informally outside of school organizations. In light of the mental boundaries typically surrounding formal process of schooling, the latter assertion is perhaps more provocative than the first. If asked, "who are educational leaders?" people tend to first reply with answers such as "principal," "teacher," or the names of other formal positions within organized systems of schooling.

Upon further discussion, however, many readers may recognize the multiple meanings associated with words like "education," "learning," and "leadership" and thus begin to conceive of broader understandings. For example, "education," can refer to either collective activity (study, research, etc.)

associated with formal institutions or to describe a single individual's path of learning over some period. And now, because we've just used the words "formal" and "learning," we have invited readers to consider (1) the possible contrasts between formal and informal and (2) comparisons between education and learning. The following section will thus discuss the contrasts and comparisons and then juxtapose them with the concept of "leadership."

Education, learning, and leading: Formal and informal

Whether one defines "leadership" in terms of mobilizing volition or advancing the solution of tasks and problems, education and learning serve as its key processes and outcomes. If education is thought of as a process in which activities and experiences are gradually assembled in some purposeful way, then it follows that "learning" serves as its units. For example, one might "learn" to play the guitar, but a musical "education" centered upon the guitar would likely consist of extended units of learning. To the extent that such learning or education were externally encouraged or directed, one may infer that some form and combination of formal and/or informal leadership had occurred.

We can now consider the connection between "formal" and "informal" in education, learning, and leadership. The formal-informal continuum has been used to draw a contrast between forms of organization that are explicitly planned to attain particular goals and other forms of organization that are mostly the result of circumstances related to individual or group needs. The classic example of this is offered by Barnard (1938) who spoke of formal organization as an established structure of planned and coordinated activity among two or more persons aimed at achieving specific results. Informal organization, he suggested however, resulted spontaneously from the coincidental collective of individuals associated with a formal organization. Informal organization, he suggested, would gradually produce its own characteristic social and normative structure capable of promoting or impeding the goals of the formal organization. Examples might include such things as the "grapevine," a useful and often important form of organizational communication. Another common example is "plea bargaining" within the U.S. judicial system – a strategy and process developed out of grassroots necessity and not found in any law book.

In more recent times, the formal-informal contrast has been applied to education and learning. The institution of schooling, either public or private, is considered a means of providing formal learning and education. Informal learning can also occur within such formal settings. Various scholars (Coleman, 1961; Dreeben, 1968; Jackson, 1968) have described in rich detail the vast amount of learning that occurs in school that is only peripherally related to classroom lessons and often related to the acceptance or inculcation of social norms. The informal social education that follows over longer periods may be vital when it comes to developing intuitive understandings of interactions and relationships; for example, who to trust, who not to trust, and how to tell the difference (Shouse, 2004).

It is also the case, however, that academic learning can occur informally – or less formally – within formal school organizations. Examples might consist of activity related to clubs, music, or athletics that allow students to apply their learned skills in a context of individual interest and choice. In addition, teachers may also encourage less formal forms of learning through the use of semi-structured "free choice" assignments or through field trips to key locations such as museums, farms, and theater.

Although the terms "informal learning" and "informal education" tend to be applied to out-of-school activity, the lines are sometimes blurry. Consider, for example, a child who develops an interest in collecting coins or stamps. The child's interest typically begins at an informal level, perhaps triggered by a friend or sibling. Learning gradually occurs as the child acquires knowledge about different nations or famous people and historic events. Over time, the child may acquire knowledge about the stamps or coins themselves – e.g., production, style, metallic content, or value. He or she may even begin to attend stamp/coin exhibitions, interact with other collectors, or become a member of a formal club. Two things have thus occurred. First, the experience shifts from one of learning to one of education. Second, what was originally an informal process interacts with and takes on characteristics of formal learning and education. Processes involving music, art, sports, politics, just to list a few, are likely to follow a similar pattern.

As further example, one of your authors volunteered to serve as an extra in a university police training film on how to react in the event of a terrorist attack on campus. Participation was both formal and informal. On one hand, involvement was casual, voluntarily, and without expectation of acquiring a great deal of skill. On the other hand, by interacting with the formally organized filming effort, knowledge of the process of constructing a set of meaningful scenes was acquired. The experience was something like a casual trip to an art museum – go for pleasure, follow a set of formal rules and routines (e.g., "do not touch," "no flash photography"), and leave having learned in a context that was self-regulated and self-evaluated.

One can also imagine processes of learning and education that are completely informal. A daughter learns to cook by watching her father do so over a long period of time. She may ask questions and he may offer advice, but most of the learning occurs with little or no systematic instruction. Indeed, many or most of the skills young people eventually develop may be learned entirely outside of school.

Leadership in formal and informal educational settings

A number of issues need to be sorted out with regard to leadership and its relation to education and learning within and outside of organizational settings. As previously suggested, "leadership" essentially refers to the "mobilization

Table 2.1 Intersections of Formality, Leader Type, and Educational Setting

Leadership type	Educational setting	
	Formal	Informal
Formal	A. School Principal	C. Piano Teacher
Informal	B. Teacher Leader	D. Parent

of volition" toward particular goals. We begin by discussing the formal and informal nature of leadership within formal and informal educational settings. Table 2.1 serves as an initial organizing framework, listing simple examples of leader types.

It appears, however, that Table 2.1 is somewhat lacking in at least two ways. First, it presents a truncated representation of "learning" and "education," which have been collapsed into the heading of "educational setting." Second, it is understood that principals, teachers, and parents vary greatly in their leadership capability and effectiveness. The following paragraphs aim at fleshing out Table 2.1 by discussing the underlying logic behind the placement of the examples within each cell.

Formal leadership in formal setting: The principal

Consider, for example, the example of "principal," here used to represent formal leadership within a formally organized setting. Although in everyday terms, one speaks of the principal as "the leader of the school," the term is typically used to designate a formal administrative or managerial position. In reality, leadership – as the ability to mobilize volition – may be more or less absent from or unnecessary to the principal's skills or responsibilities. As others have argued (Selznick, 1959; Shouse & Lin, 2010), leadership (as mobilized volition toward change) may sometimes be "dispensable" or unnecessary.

Informal leadership in formal settings: The teacher

"Teacher" is used to represent informal leadership within formal organization. Teachers, of course, have a formal leadership role, that of leading students; to mobilize classroom volition toward the act of learning. The informal teacher-leader role involves the mobilization of volition beyond the classroom into the realm of professional practice. Although this can take a wide range of shapes and sizes, one typical case might involve the public expression (and implicitly the mobilization) of opposition and resistance to the imposition of rules or regulations perceived to impose on teachers' professional judgments.

Over time, teachers may yield a substantial amount of symbolic or strategic influence with colleagues, which in some instances can create sufficient power to block top-down organizational initiatives or directives. Such situations illustrate the potential for conflict between formal and informal authority when representatives of each disagree over the size and shape of the organizational zone of acceptance. Indeed, the ability of organizational collectives to expand this zone is evidence that "leadership" has occurred.

Formal leadership in informal settings: The piano teacher

Many teachers, of course, operate primarily outside of or adjacent to formally organized settings. Consider, for instance, the neighbor down the street who offers piano lessons to local children. The educational setting may be entirely unconnected to any formal organization. Seldom are contracts involved and lesson times are flexible and subject to change. Evaluation tends to be cordial, intrinsic, and absent of significant external reward or sanction. The actual teaching, however, occurs in coordinated and regularized fashion following a specific predesigned course of study. Teachers may assign homework, expect a certain standard of performance to be met, and engage in a range of strategies to improve student performance and increase motivation. Because progression to advanced skill levels is often very frustrating for students, and because attrition rates may be quite high, successful teaching depends on an ability to persuade students to suspend their own judgment in favor of the teacher's. That is, it depends on the teacher's ability to mobilize the volition of students who may perceive their involvement as casual or temporary.

Informal leadership in informal settings: The parent

A great deal of parenting can be understood as the exercise of informal leadership in informal educational settings. It is true, of course that parents possess formal legal authority over their children and that a family can be understood as both formal institution and structure. It is also true that parents may adopt relatively formal, regularized, and coordinated forms of teaching and guidance, with examples being things like regular church attendance, family meetings, or requiring a child to attend a drug rehabilitation camp. At the same time, a tremendous amount of parental teaching and guidance occurs informally. For example, though parents may wish a child to acquire various skills and attributes (i.e., housework, musical skill, honesty, responsibility, good overall character), much of the teaching and guidance associated with this kind of learning takes place informally through example, suggestion, or as particular problems or opportunities arise. Whatever learning that results from such informal interaction tends to be voluntary on the part of the child; that is, the long-term job of education and guidance hinges on the parent's ability to

32 Impossible mission II

expand their child's zone of acceptance through strategies varying in quality, consistency, and effectiveness.

The examples and explanations above on leadership within education and learning settings may be applicable to non-Western societies. In China, as discussed in concurrent essays, the idea of leadership, or *lingdao*, tends to be limited to actions taken within the context of formal position and formal organization (type A in Table 2.1). Shouse and Lin's (2010) observations from Taiwan are also applicable throughout China; that (1) "school leaders" are those with formal authority, (2) the principal holds the highest position of authority, and (3) and "leadership" flows in one direction (downwardly toward subordinates). Yet, as we've pointed out, numerous elements exist within Chinese literature and history emphasizing non-formal contributions of individual citizens to various social and political initiatives both within and outside of formal organization or position (see Table 2.1, types B, C, and D). Mandarin language nevertheless contains no single explicit term to capture the idea of "informal leader."

From an anthropological perspective, this poses no "problem." Rather, it may be interpreted as reflecting the collectivist, power-distance dispositions of East Asian culture (Hofstede, 1991). From a sociolinguistic view, however, words and meanings are socially constructed, often disconnected from actual phenomena. This disconnect led us to discover the writings of Ferdinand de Saussure on relationships between "thoughts" and "sounds." Writing in the early 20th century (Harris, 1990), he stated that

> Words are not mere vocal labels or communicational adjuncts superimposed upon an already given order of things. They are collective products of social interaction, essential instruments through which human beings constitute and articulate their world.

His idea seems to be fit and helpful in understanding the puzzling situation we have been discussing. It supports our point that leadership – and educational leadership – is fundamentally natural and informal process of human survival, which has migrated and evolved within formal organizational settings. This idea thus opens the door to the problematization (Crotty, 1998) of what could be called the East Asian leadership myth – the formalistic, top-down, and nested understanding of what it means to lead.

Figures 2.2 and 2.3 offer further support for and illustration of these arguments, suggesting the loose connections between "ideas" and "sounds." The top irregular area (A) indicates ideas and thoughts within the society; the bottom irregular area (B) indicates vocalized sounds or words. Between the two is a "nether region" in which the connections between the two are socially or politically negotiated or contested. The vertical lines map the rough associations of thoughts and sounds. Language combines the elements of sound

Impossible mission II 33

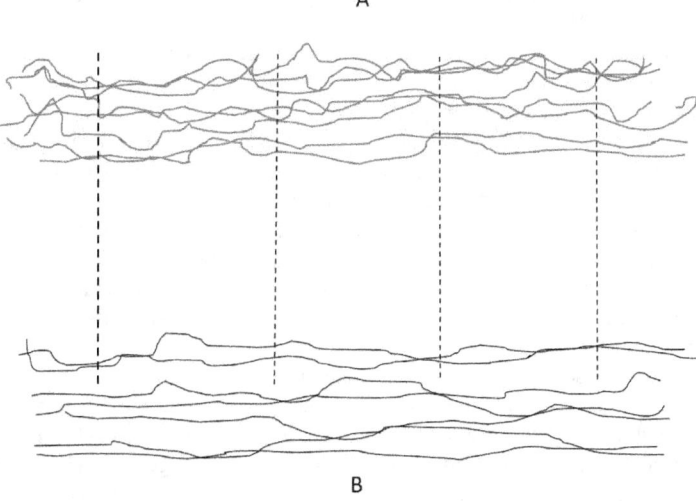

Figure 2.2 Ideas (A) and Sounds (B) (From Hansen, 2001, Following Saussure, 1916/1959)

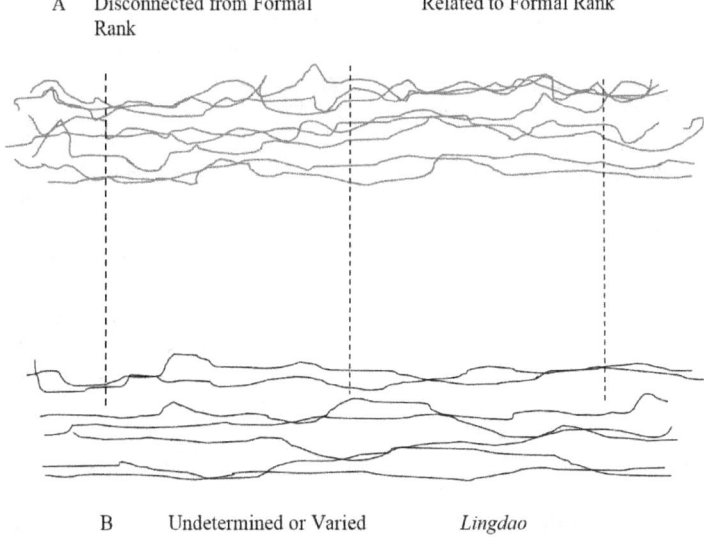

Figure 2.3 Sociolinguistic Negotiation (Time 1)

and thought and produces, as Saussure emphasized, "a form, not a substance" (Hansen, 2001).

In our present case, Figure 2.2 suggests how the human mind can observe, imagine, and connect numerous combinations of individuals, actions, and assigned labels related to purposes of mobilizing collective volition; what we refer to here (for simplicity's sake) as "leadership." However, between the mind's conception and its corresponding word lies a playing field of social interaction and linguistic negotiation over various time frames. At the present time, for example, negotiation within the Chinese social framework has resulted in *lingdao* being assigned specifically to individuals, actions, and intents associated with formal rank and authority. Similar actions and intents conducted by individuals outside of formal rank are left with no simple corresponding word (see Figure 2.3).

From a sociolinguistic perspective, negotiation does not cease and meaning is continually contested. Today, moreover, the contest has shifted to a global arena, even to the words of songwriters: Paul Simon's "lasers in the jungle" and Laurie Andersons' "language" as "virus." In other words, the construction of meaning now transcends national or cultural boundaries. Local structures of meaning can no longer be considered sacrosanct.

The role of cinema

Our proposed study will explore the ways in which popular film serves to extend and redefine the meaning of *lingdao* so as to represent the mobilization of volition by groups and individuals outside of formal positions of authority. Film is a language – a virus – and a powerful global resource challenging and reconstructing connections between ideas and language.

As explicit narrative and implicit symbol, film has the potential to reshape both individual and social understandings of power distance, political efficacy, and, ultimately, connections between ideas and language. Cinematic narratives can potentially deconstruct, negotiate, and reconstruct viewers' opinion, imagination, and sense of agency. In short, by revealing acts of determination and courage, the film depicts *lingdao* and invites viewers to conceive of it in new ways. A good example of this is the film *Pretty Big Feet*, the story of a strong and independent woman who constantly struggled to persuade her small, drought-plagued village that education offered the only means for community survival. Through wit, determination, and sacrifice, Teacher Zhang overcomes traditional barriers of male dominance and the attraction of distant urban life to raise the educational consciousness of her students and other villagers. At the same time, the film aims to raise the social consciousness of the audience, reminding them of their debt and obligation to those who struggle to improve the nation. *Zhang Lao Shi* (Teacher Zhang) becomes a symbol and a tool for mobilizing volition among citizens and educators.

Impossible mission II 35

One thus sees how film constructs *lingdao* in multiple ways – through the actions of characters, through its overall message, and through its very creation by the collective individuals responsible for these. An important task for researchers of educational leadership then is to decode the meaning that flows from creative production, to big-screen images, to social transmission. To put it in slightly different terms, the messages within a film can change the minds of those who view it; but the release and distribution of a film can potentially change an entire nation. Effective films can arrange events and narratives to generate audience identification, empathy, and understanding – to create entirely new patterns of thought and language that can become diffused throughout a society. Figure 2.4 suggests the capability of film (as process and as product) to rearrange connections between ideas and language.

Film works as a powerful negotiator between ideas, images, and language, and a catalyst for interaction between critical issues, social phenomena,

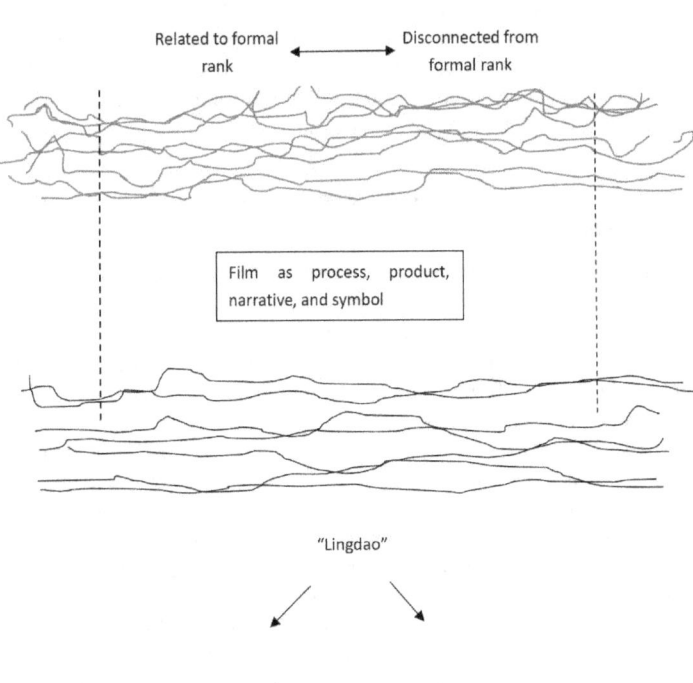

Figure 2.4 Sociolinguistic Negotiation (Time 2)

individuals, and society. This negotiation (i.e., creation, distribution, viewing, and impact) evolves and is understood formally or informally depending on time and circumstance. An original film idea, for instance, may come from the mind of an artist or writer (informal), while the subsequent technical and distribution processes will tend to occur in some sort of formally organized setting. If the film is historical, it may become a required part of an academic course, in which case the "leading and learning" also occur within a formal framework. Most of the time, however, decisions to view and/or be influenced by a film are informal. The issue of sanction or censorship adds another layer of complexity, as a state or other formal interests may authorize or seek to restrict the creation or viewing of a film.

In terms of educational outcome, film evolves like "organized anarchy" – issues are problematic, technology is uncertain, and participation is fluid (Cohen et al., 1972). Narratives are deciphered and understood in different ways, even differently from the creators' original intent. Of course, the same is true for many other creative works such as literature, music, painting, or even conversations between people.

As researchers, we also contribute to the process, proposing and eventually placing this study in the space between thought and language. The answers and ideas we offer are intended to promote further discussion; in other words, to propose the word *lingdao* to the mobilization of volition outside of formal position is not a solution or an end to a problem. Rather, it is a way of generating new thoughts and new understanding.

Grammar, syntax, and the cinematic construction of meaning

Clifford Solway (1966) states that a film is "a didactic arrangement of camera shots, charged with meanings and implications nowhere in the original, organized for cumulative impact." Directors and producers use film as a pliable medium for sending out messages and meaning. In this study of leadership, film meaning is interpreted in two ways. First, films are viewed as texts depicting the contributions of individual citizens working informally (without official position or authority) in pursuit of social goals through manifest acts of persuasion, an activity commonly understood in Western society as attempted leadership. Second, the authorization, construction, and distribution of the film itself is also viewed as a manifest act of social persuasion. According to McLuhan and Fiore's (1967) important idea "the medium is the message," a "medium embeds itself in the message, creating a symbiotic relationship by which the medium influences how the message is perceived." Thus, the film, as medium, serves as a focus of leadership study because of its potential to reshape social meanings not only via explicit text but also by the characteristics of the film itself.

A key task of this study, then, is to interpret meanings embedded in the images on the big screen to understand the "leadership activity" portrayed within a sample of Chinese films, as well as that represented by the directors, producers, and others responsible for their creation. To put it in slightly different terms, the messages within a film can change the minds of those who view it; but the release and distribution of a film can potentially change an entire nation. Effective films can arrange events and narratives to generate audience identification, empathy, and understanding – to create entirely new patterns of affect and intellect which then become diffused throughout a society. Through the manipulation of events, characters, sounds, and story, a skilled director can lead an audience to experience a noble or heroic struggle similar to that expressed within the film.

In order to capture and analyze both types of leadership phenomena, a major concern of the study is to decode the grammar and syntax of the film and find out how the ordering and arrangement of shots and scenes contribute to the construction of leadership meanings. Within the selected films, various techniques have been used to stress or symbolize characteristics and activities of leadership. As Fabe (2004) suggests in *Closely Watched Films: An Introduction to the Art of Narrative Film Technique*, shots manipulation can be grouped under the headings of editing, duration, type, camera movement, camera angle, camera lens, lighting, composition, symbolism, and sound.

In addition, the director's choice and use of actors, choice of setting or set design, props, costumes, and make-up also influence the credibility of a film in the eyes of its viewers (Fabe, 2004). Thus, the "mise-en-scène" (the cinematography and other assorted visual themes to which viewers are introduced) help express meaning, time and space, and bring the audience into the action and experience of the main characters. First, we will explain in general how some these techniques can influence the viewing experience of the audience; in particular, how they work to reinforce a leadership message in the film. We will then illustrate the influence of these techniques using one of the films in the present study's data base to show how leadership traits have been intentionally attributed to the characters and how the director tried to lead the audience by sending out messages.

Summary

Chapters 1 and 2 were designed to describe the conceptual puzzle of leadership meaning in the Chinese context and to argue that meanings attached to *Lingdao*, though solidly associated with formal rank, could be problematized and social negotiated through the creation and presentation of cinematic counter-narratives. These two chapters offered rationale for this position, along with descriptions of a potential framework for film analysis. The following chapter will provide more details of the sample selection and analytic methods to be used in this study.

References

Barnard, C. (1938). *The functions of the executive*. Harvard University.
Bredeson, P. V., & Kose, B. W. (2007). Responding to the education reform agenda: A study of school superintendents' instructional leadership. *Education Policy Analysis Archives*, *15*, 5–5.
Bush, T., & Qiang, H. (2002). Leadership and culture in Chinese education. In A. Walker, & C. Dimmock (Eds.), *School leadership and administration: Adopting a cultural perspective* (pp. 173–186). Routledge Falmer.
Carlson, D. (2003). Troubling heroes: Of Rosa Parks, multicultural education, and critical pedagogy. *Cultural Studies? Critical Methodologies*, *3*(1), 44–61.
Chen, M. (1995). *Asian Management systems: Chinese, Japanese and Korean styles of business*. Routledge.
Cohen, M. D., March, J. G., & Olsen, J. P. (1972). A garbage can model of organizational choice. *Administrative Science Quarterly*, *17*(1), 1–25.
Coleman, J. S. (1961). *The adolescent society*. The Free Press.
Cremin, L. A. (1988). *American education: The metropolitan experience, 1876–1980*. Harper and Row.
Crotty, M. J. (1998). *Foundations of social research: Meaning and perspective in the research process*. Sage Publications.
Dreeben, R. (1968). *On what is learned in school*. Addison-Wesley.
Fabe, M. (2004). *Closely watched films: An introduction to the art of narrative film technique*. University of California Press.
Fairhurst, G. (2007). *Discursive leadership: In conversation with leadership psychology*. Sage.
Haller, E. J., & Strike, K. A. (1986). *An introduction to educational administration: Social, legal, and ethical perspectives*. Addison-Wesley Longman.
Hansen, G. P. (2001). *The trickster and the paranormal*. Xlibris Corp.
Harris, R. (1990). *Language, Saussure and Wittengenstein*: How to play games with words. ix. Routledge.
Hemphill, J. K. (1949). *Situational factors in leadership*. Ohio State University, Bureau of Educational Research Monograph.
Herbert, A. S. (1957). *Administrative behavior: A study of decision-making processes in administrative organization*. Free Press.
Hofstede, G. (1991). Empirical models of cultural differences. In N. Gleichrodt & P. Drenth (Eds.), *Contemporary issues in cross-cultural psychology* (pp. 4–20). Swets & Zeitlinger.
Hofstede, G., Hofstede, G. J., & Minkov, M. (1991). *Cultures and organizations: Software of the mind* (Vol. 2). McGraw-Hill.
Hong, J., & Engeström, Y. (2004). Changing principles of communication between Chinese managers and workers Confucian authority chains and guanxi as social networking. *Management Communication Quarterly*, *17*(4), 552–585.
Hoy, W. K., & Miskel, C. G. (2001). *Educational administration: Theory, research, and practice*. McGraw-Hill.
Jackson, P. W. (1968). *Life in classrooms*. Teachers College Press.
Katz, D., & Kahn, R. L. (1966). *The social psychology of organizations*. John Wiley & Sons Inc.
Law, W. W. (2012). Educational leadership and culture in China: Dichotomies between Chinese and Anglo-American leadership traditions? *International Journal of Educational Development*, *32*(2), 273–282.

Mao, Y. (2011). Educational discourse in film: The history of Chinese educational documentaries. *Front Education China*, *6*(4), 620–638. doi: 10.1007/s11516-011-0148-9.

McGurk, P. (2009). Developing "middle leaders" in the public services? The realities of management and leadership development for public managers. *International Journal of Public Sector Management*, *22*(6), 464–477.

McLuhan, M., & Fiore, Q. (1967). *The medium is the message*. Routledge.

Robinson, V. M. (2001). Embedding leadership in task performance. In K. Wong & C. Evers, Leadership for quality schooling: International perspectives (90–100). Routledge.

Selznick, P. (1957). *Leadership in administration: A sociological interpretation*. Harper & Row.

Selznick, P. (1959). Sociology of law. *The Journal of Legal Education*, *12*, 521.

Shah, S. (2006). Educational leadership: An Islamic perspective. *British Educational Research Journal*, *32*(3), 363–385.

Shouse, R. C. (2004). Democratic spirit and moral learning. In F. Hammack (Ed.), *The Comprehensive High School Today* (pp. 69–86). Teachers College.

Shouse, R. C. (2005). Taking Lulu seriously: What we can learn from "To Sir with Love. *Journal of Educational Administration*, *43*(4), 357–367.

Shouse, R. C. (2009). Beyond legend: Stand and Deliver as a study in school organizational culture. *Film & History an Interdisciplinary Journal of Film and Television Studies*, *39*(1), 45–52.

Shouse, R. C., & Lin, K. P. (2010). *Principal leadership in Taiwan schools*. Rowman & Littlefield Publishers.

Shouse, R. C., & Ma, C. (2015). Leadership and creativity in East Asian schools. *Asia Pacific Education Review*, *16*, 491–499.

Sia, A. (1997). *The Chinese art of leadership*. Asiapac.

Solway, C. (1966). Film, television, and reality. *The Teachers College Record*, *68*(3), 197–199.

Spillane, J. P. (2004). Educational leadership. *Educational Evaluation and Policy Analysis*, *26*(2), 169–172.

Thomas, R. A. (1998). As they are portrayed: Principals in film. *International Journal of Educational Management*, *12*(2), 90–100.

Wang, T. (2007). Understanding Chinese educational leaders' conceptions in an international education context. *International Journal of Leadership in Education*, *10*(1), 71–88. doi: 10.1080/13603120500445275.

Wang, X. (2009). Three trends in recent studies of modern Chinese literature and culture. *China Perspectives*, *80*, 118.

Wang, B. X., & Chee, H. (2011). *Chinese leadership*. Palgrave Macmillan.

Wehmeier, S. (2004). *Oxford advanced learner's English-Chinese dictionary*. The Commercial Press and Oxford University Press.

Wong, K. C. (2001). Chinese culture and leadership. *International Journal of Leadership in Education*, *4*(4), 309–319. doi: 10.1080/13603120110077990.

Yukl, G. (1998). *Leadership in organisations* (4th ed.). Prentice Hall.

Zhou, X. L. (2009). Screening education: Schools on film in the People's Republic of China. *Sungkyun Journal of East Asian Studies*, *9*(2), 213–230.

3 Impossible mission III
To pitch films displaying discursive leadership

The various broad and perhaps non-traditional understandings of leadership discussed in previous chapters prompted us to consider non-traditional approaches to support their legitimacy within an East Asian context. Having viewed ample examples of "untethered" leadership themes in a wide range of American popular film, we searched for comparable examples in Chinese cinema, particularly within contexts of education and schooling. Specifically, to what extent did such cinematic texts depict or imply "Western" understandings of leadership?

Data sources

For purposes of this book, "Chinese cinematic texts" are understood to comprise two broad categories of fictional or non-fictional/documentary films depicting Chinese cultural, social, organizational, or political themes and served to the public as a communicative artifact as "visual rhetoric" (Foss, 2004). According to the definition given by Sonja. K. Foss (2004), visual rhetoric has two senses of meaning which could mean both a visual object and a perspective on the study of visual data. In the first sense, visual rhetoric is a product individuals create as they use visual symbols for the purpose of communicating. In the second, it is a perspective scholars apply that focuses on the symbolic processes by which visual artifacts perform communication (Foss, 2004).

Thus, through the medium of their products, filmmakers and producers tend to communicate with the audience by enciphering various codes and visual symbols into their films and other video products.

In this case, it is important to figure out how filmmakers express and depict behaviors, actions, or characters involved in mobilization of collective volition within Chinese education environment. What's the message they want to communicate with the public through the film as visual rhetoric? Did the films bring any change or influence on the lives of characters or audiences? With these questions as guiding principles, we accessed published lists of the movies released each year between 1979 and 2013,

DOI: 10.4324/9781032723778-4

works created after the Cultural Revolution and less likely to be shaped by propaganda.

Within the Chinese film data base, there are basically two category of films under the supervision of the State Administration of Radio Film and Television (SARFT). One category consists of "authorized" works, films produced in China, typically by Chinese filmmakers, and approved for mass commercial distribution and viewing within the PRC. A second category consists of films of similar genre, created, distributed, or viewed without SARFT authorization. Within this study, both the authorized and non-authorized films fitting our criteria have been considered. Such films consisted of a variety of genres, fiction, historic, documentary, and pseudo-documentary appearing to convey condensed experience to viewers.

Sample selection criteria

After determined the data source of this research, several sample selection criteria were specified and carried out in accordance to provide relative and useful data to the research questions efficiently. First, we examined portrayals of characters "worthy of remembrance" in terms of mobilizing collective volition in discourse, behavior, interaction, and the consequences of their actions on themselves and others. We then selected films and documentaries known to be famous or influential in terms of recording or causing social changes within Chinese society. To be specific, we examined films that portrayed real-life events or experience during tremendous social change periods of China. These would have included depictions from ancient to current time. Also included were films that had caught public's attention, appeared to have had social influence, or those with strong persuasive and/or symbolic messages. Many of the films we considered had been heatedly discussed on various online movie forums, such as Douban Movie (one of the most popular film review websites in China), Internet Movie Data Base (IMDB), and Rotten Tomatoes, both within and beyond China's boundaries. Lastly, educational settings were considered a preferable but not necessary criteria for the film selection.

Sample selection

After surveying Chinese and Chinese-related films dating back to 1979, based on the selection criteria, we constructed a list of films that appeared to illustrate examples of informal leadership/discursive leadership in Chinese society (see Table 3.1).

The films listed in Table 3.1 were selected based on their focused portrayal of characters and/or events engaged in or related to acts of change, struggle, or persuasion and in which the characters are portrayed as heroic, honorable,

Table 3.1 List of Films Depicting Informal Leadership in Chinese Educational Settings

Film title	Date	Type	Authorized	Setting
King of the Children	1987	F	Y	Substitute teacher, rural school
Her Smile Through Candlelight	1991	F	Y	Teacher, poor-quality Shanghai school
The Blue Kite	1993	F	N	Middle-class family through recent Chinese history
Long Ji	1994	D	Y	Rural students
*Country Teachers	1994	F	Y	Teachers in rural village school
The Grass House	1998	F	Y	Principal, middle-class elementary school
*Not One Less	1999	F	Y	Substitute teacher, poor rural school
A Student Village	1999	D	Y	Remote, rural boarding school
The Shining Teenagers	2002	F	Y(TV)	High school teacher befriends students
Balzac and the Little Chinese Seamstress	2002	F	N	Displaced students befriend peasant girl, Cultural Revolution
*Pretty Big Feet	2003	F	Y	Principal, poor rural elementary school
*Senior Year	2005	D	Y	Dynamic high school teacher, college entrance exam
Little Red Flowers	2006	F	Y	Nonconforming student at Chinese pre-school
Substitute Teachers	2006	F	Y	Displaced, struggling rural teachers
Thirteen Princess Trees	2006	F	Y	Disaffected high school youth, teacher corruption
My Career as a Teacher	2007	F	Y	Displaced rural teacher clashes with principal
*Please Vote for Me	2007	D	N	Third-grade students campaign for class presidency
Angel's Heart	2007	F	Y	Struggles of rural students and teachers
Feng Zhiyuan	2007	F	Y	Hard-working teacher, 1950s Shanghai, loses eyesight
Chinese Schools	2008	D	Y(TV)	Focus on daily life inside China's school system
Apology	2008	F	Y	Principal's struggle to change student's attitude
The Call of Maiji Mount	2011	F	Y	Teacher returns to her own rural school
*Education, Education	2012	F	N	Disreputable colleges revealed
Mark of Youth	2013	F	Y	Teachers strive for friendly relationships with students

(*Continued*)

Table 3.1 (Continued)

Film title	Date	Type	Authorized	Setting
Children at a Village School	2014	D	Y	Teacher strives for Liushou (Left at home) children's study and life
After School	2017	F	Y	Reporter tries to set up after school childcare service
Looking up	2019	F	Y	Father homeschooling child makes difference

*Films selected for in-depth written analysis.
Bold type indicates original viewed sample.

or worthy of remembrance. Based on this framework, the sample of films was selected as follows:

- films familiar to the authors that fit the above criteria and/or
- films dealing with issues related to educational and/or social change in China, obtained from an internet search.
- films recommended by others during the time of data collection.

Narrowing of sample

Based on film availability and to avoid repetition of themes, ten films were selected for in-depth viewing (listed in bold type in Table 3.1). After consideration of overall content and relevance, six films were selected for in-depth written analysis in this chapter: *Pretty Big Feet*[1] (2003), *Senior Year*[2] (2005), *Not One Less*[3] (1999), *Please Vote for Me*[4] (2007), *Education, Education*[5] (2012), and *Country Teachers*[6] (1994).

Analytic approach

Mass media, such as movies and television shows, are a collection of images deliberately designed by production teams to convey ideas to audience. More specifically, it is common for producers to do so to encourage diverse ideas and voice as a means of promoting social changes or, at least, changes in public mindscapes (Hill & Helmers, 2012). To infer the "existence of images, emotions, and ideas" (Foss, 2004) within a visual artifact, purposeful combinations of colors, lines, textures, and rhythm need to be noted and analyzed.

To gather the needed information from the data source, inductive content analysis served as the main analytic approach for our study. As Harold Lasswell (1948) noted, the essence and main effort of content analysis is to understand "who says what, to whom, why, to what extent and with what effect?" Or, as Kimberly Neuendorf (2002, p. 10) explains, content analysis is,

> ...a summarising, quantitative analysis of messages that ... is not limited as to the types of variables that may be measured or the context in which the messages are created or presented.

Thus, the major components of conducting inductive content analysis within this study are as follows: (1) documents, which included cinematic and literary texts about filmmakers, (2) data coding, organization, and deciphering symbols and other visual and audio rhetoric within the texts, and (3) weaving these elements together into a comprehensive craftwork.

Data collection and coding

Films were first viewed and examined with an eye toward scenes, events, and concrete or symbolic acts suggesting the mobilizing of collective volition. Notes were taken and codes were developed to categorize emerging themes related to informal expressions of leadership, authority, and power.

Character quotes, thick descriptions of film events, and detailed observational notes were gathered as data entry and placed in a research journal using Beyerbach's (2005) film data organizational method. Table 3.2 illustrates a typical data entry of the cinematic texts as data source.

Next, relevant and influential evidence regarding film grammar and syntax via shooting techniques such as shot type and duration, camera movement and angle, lens selection, lighting, and sound were recorded and analyzed to understand if and how the filmmakers aimed to create a values-driven, audience-receptive context.

Shot duration

The length (duration) of shots is an important consideration that can greatly affect the rhythm or pace of the film. Based on the editing of film shots, the "storyteller" weaves information and messages across scenes to convey desired meaning. Long shots are associated with more relaxing and lyrical moments. Short shots traditionally being used to show urgent, emergent, and even violent scenes.

Shots that end before viewers can fully understand all they contain, such as sudden cuts or fade outs, can instill nervousness, anxiety, or excitement. In contrast, shots that shift after sufficient viewer comprehension tend to invoke calm, contemplation, or boredom (Fabe, 2004). Thus, when characters are captured in shots with a shorter duration or sudden fades, audiences may perceive a more intense environment invoking a need for urgent leadership or action.

Table 3.2 Example of Data Entry for Pretty Big Feet

Film title	Pretty Big Feet
Context	Set in a small northwest China village on the Loess Plateau
Storyline	• Ms. Zhang Meili, a strong and independent woman, who believed that education was the only way to help the villages change their fate, set up a school in the dry desert landscape of northwest China. • The movie centers on three relationships – the communication between Zhang and a Beijing volunteer teacher Xia Yu; the intimacy/love affair between Zhang and Wang Shu, the village projectionist; and the special commitment by the two teachers to the village's children.
Attempted informal leadership portrayed in the film	1. Ms. Zhang is a non-traditional woman who struggled to break through the traditional shackles through the power of knowledge as a teacher and a principal. 2. Ms. Zhang is also a determined person who sticks to her dream – to provide better education and a bright future to the kids. And her persistent and never-give-up attitude on the kids and on the education career finally moved Ms. Xia and changed her mind. 3. Ms. Zhang is the altruistic mother figure in the film. Her dedication and selflessness have strongly moved and influenced the surrounding people, especially the kids and people close to her.
Discursive leadership (i.e., the film's overall moral or social message)	1. All you affluent city folk need to understand all the sacrifice and devotion that took place historically so that you could have a "soft life". 2. You still have an obligation to help your brothers and sisters who are less fortunate than you. 3. Poverty people in the rural areas tried hard to make a living deserve to be respected and given help by the affluent city folks. 4. Education as the major way of changing the living condition of the rural people should be emphasized and is paid more attention to by the government.
Emerging themes	1. Activity related to a lot of sacrifice, devotion, and obligation. 2. Emphasis of persistence of hard work, selflessness. 3. Leadership exercised through emotional attachment. 4. Demonstrating the value of education.

Shot type

Different types of shots and framing may also generate different emotional or intellectual feelings, experiences, and responses among an audience. The most common shot types are introduced in Table 3.3 with film Pretty Big Feet as sample data.

Table 3.3 Varieties of Cinematic Shots – e.g., Pretty Big Feet

Shot name	Shooting technique	Shot effect	Example (from film Pretty Big Feet)[7]
Extreme long shot (ELS)/ Extreme wide shot (EWS)	Extreme long (wide) shots are far removed from subject; often shot with wide-angle lens.	ELS may show subject in distance, but emphasis is on showing subject in his/her environment.	ELS shows droughty and barren environment to express isolation.
Long shot (LS)/Wide shot (WS)	Long shots (also known as wide shots) provide overall view of scene.	Sometimes called an establishing shot; orients audience as to location, weather, time of the day, etc.	WS establishes character's action, surrounding environment.
Medium shot (MS)	Medium shot shows interaction between characters, including dialog.	MS shows movement and background info while still focused on subject.	Interaction between two characters had been greatly captured by MS.
Close up (CU)	Close-up shots typically show the face and shoulders of a subject, with some headroom.	CU shots convey emotion and help audience connect with the subject. Used to reveal character's thoughts and feelings.	CU shot shows determination and dedication to lead students.

(*Continued*)

Table 3.3 (Continued)

Shot name	Shooting technique	Shot effect	Example (from film Pretty Big Feet)[7]
Extreme close up (ECU)	ECU focuses on particular part of a person, object, or animal.	ECU shots create intimacy, mood, or emotion. Focus on significance.	ECU on feet shows symbolic meaning.
Reaction shot (RS)	RS (or noddy shot), show listening or reacting.	Shows effect of one person's words or actions on other people in the scene.	Scene shows a cheerful response.
Point of view shot (POV)	POV (first person or subjective shot) shows character perspective.	Audience assumes character's position and perception to create sense of identification.	POV from child's angle, with emphasis on bracelet.

Camera movement

In a movie, the direction of lens movement can have a dramatic effect on viewers. The most common camera movements are the pan shot, swish pan, tilt, traveling shot, and crane shot. One famous example of how meaning can be created this way is the crane shot scene from the 1952 film *High Noon*. Director Fred Zinneman pulls the camera upward and away from Marshal Kane, showing him alone, isolated, and in danger on his town's main street.

Camera angle

Camera angle variation can give factual, experiential, or emotional information to the audience and guide their judgment about the characters or objects in shot (see Table 3.4). Extreme angles, for instance, can emphasize one character's power over others in the film. The more extreme the angle, the more

48 *Impossible mission III*

Table 3.4 Varieties of Angle Shots – e.g., Pretty Big Feet

Shot angle name	Shooting technique	Shot effect	Example (Pretty Big Feet)[8]
Bird's eye view	Shot from directly overhead, a very unnatural and strange angle.	Puts audience in god-like position, looking down on action. People seem insignificant, ant-like, part of a wider scheme of things.	Bird's eye view suggests helpless, desperate feeling of crowd.
High angle	Overhead shot, not as extreme as BEV.	High angles make object seem smaller, less significant. Often used to suggest vulnerability.	High-angle shot; characters seem weak and vulnerable.
Eye level	Camera positioned from human perspective.	Expresses neutral or calm attitude.	Shot suggests harmonious relationship of two characters.
Low angle	Camera is down low looking up at character.	Low angles make subjects seem larger, imposing, or more important.	Low angle suggests character importance to the viewer.

symbolic and heavily loaded the shot. The most common camera angles are introduced in Table 3.4 with film *Pretty Big Feet* as sample data.

Lens selection

Lenses can alter the perceived magnification, depth, perspective, and scale of objects in the shot, allowing directors to shape story meaning or direction. The most common lens styles include wide-angle, fish-eye, telephoto, zoom, deep focus, soft focus, rack focus, and normal lens.

Table 3.5 Use of Lighting Techniques – e.g., Pretty Big Feet[9]

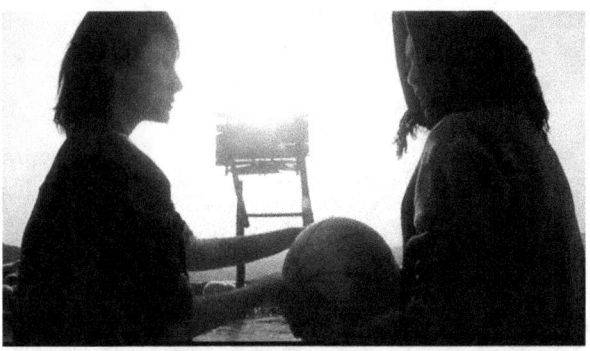

Sunlight in background indicates hope, future, expectation for new life

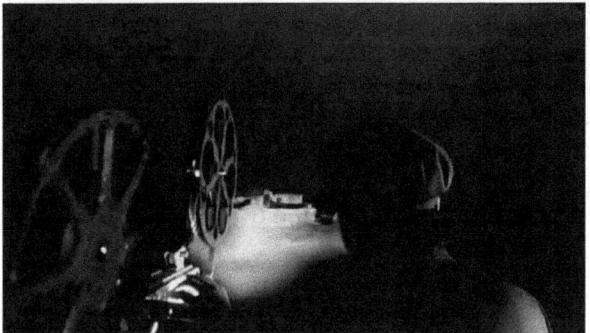

Projector light shines on school building suggests village's bright future thanks to Ms. Zhang

Lighting and color

Special application of light and color helps to draw the eye to the object of greatest significance. This is another shooting technique that can gently guide the audience's thoughts and emotions to a particular place, idea, or status. Table 3.5 lists two scenes in which the filmmaker used lighting and color to guide the audience *Pretty Big Feet*.

Sound

In modern film, sound plays an increasingly important role in creating additional levels of meaning and sensual and emotional stimuli that increase the range, depth, and intensity of audience experience. Basically, there are three categories of sound in film: dialog, sound effects, and musical score. Examples of these are offered in Table 3.6.

Table 3.6 The Creation of Meaning of Films – e.g., Pretty Big Feet

Via action	To "lead" her village, Zhang lao shi took several actions.
	• Started the only school in her village, serving as both teacher and principal.
	• Went to every household in town to promote school enrollment.
	• Raised funds by "drinking" with a rich businessman and selling potatoes grown in their village in the big city.
Via words	Zhang lao shi's anguished and compelling speech to her students (see Chapter 4) emphasizes the importance of study by appealing to their senses of shame and pride.
Via lighting	Film's final scene; "Film Wang" aims projector beam at school; signifies village's bright future, thanks to Ms. Zhang.
Via integrated scene/dialog	Word, scenery, background music signify character's importance; at 01:00:30, a red glow suddenly appears and expands one horizon; "I knew the sun will rise soon."
Via shooting techniques	Several close-up and extreme close ups of Zhang Meili and her feet;
	• Reference to movie title.
	• Symbol of her personality, worldview, and life situation.
	• Reference to Chinese foot binding, negative beliefs about big feet, women.
	• Zhang's shame over her big feet, loss of husband.
	• Zhang represents rural women of new era, struggle against bigotry.
	• Signifies Zhang's persistent hard work to improve student and village life.
	Dramatic pullback of camera at start of film;
	• Ms. Zhang and students welcome teacher Xia, camera pulls back to view them among barren mountains; Zhang's arms open widely.
Via sound	Music and songs throughout film;
	• At the start, kids do not know/can't sing the welcome song; one student, Wang Dahe, son of "Film Wang," knew the words because, as his friend said, "he is smart and he's got a father able to project films." Suggests power of knowledge and technology in this poorly educated and isolated village.
	• Ballad sung at start and end of film resonates the message and reinforce the viewer's sympathies; Wang Dahe changes words to honor Teacher Zhang.

(*Continued*)

Table 3.6 (Continued)

Via other symbols	"**Teaching stick**" represents the responsibility and authority as a teacher. "Class, Ms. Xia will be teaching you from today, let's welcome her. Ms. Xia, I am passing this teaching stick to you now (With serious expression on Zhang Meili's face)." Sunglasses and leather coats on city dwellers suggest affluence, power. **Names of the main characters**: "**Zhang Meili**" • "Mei li" means beauty in Chinese; her beautiful heart • "Mei li" also in movie's Mandarin title, "Mei Li De Da Jiao." Does it mean the big feet of Zhang Meili? Her pretty feet? That her shoes are hard to fill? "**Xia Yu**," the young visiting teacher, has the same pronunciation as "raining" in Chinese. Ms. Xia "watered" the kids with knowledge and love. Her appearance was just like a timely rain bringing hope to a remote arid village that desperately needed rain.

The techniques described above were found in most of the films selected for our study. Table 3.6 offers examples of these techniques along with other examples of how films "lead" viewers toward new understandings of social problems. For example, by highlighting the noble heroic voice of its main character (Teacher Zhang Meili) toward the film's climax, *Pretty Big Feet* uses sound as a means of audience persuasion.

Though the tone of the film is somewhat depressing and often negative, the director still aims to express a hopeful message regarding the village, its school, and Teacher Zhang's role in their positive development. The film aims to raise the social consciousness of the audience, reminding them of their debt and obligation to those who struggle to improve the nation. *Zhang Lao Shi* (Teacher Zhang Meili) becomes a symbol and a tool for mobilizing volition among citizens and educators. In order to send out the message, the movie puts much emphasis on color, light, scene setting, empty space, and various hidden symbols.

Summary

In addition to analyzing and decoding messages in cinematic texts, literary texts including news reports, interviews, and comments about film directors and/or other figure salient to either film creation process or post-release public response were gathered and analyzed as another main data source of this study. Table 3.7 illustrates a typical data entry of the literature texts of the book as data source.

Table 3.7 Example of Literature Data Entry – e.g., Pretty Big Feet

Film title	*Pretty Big Feet*
Producing team	Filmmaker: Yang Yazhou Producer: Song Dai, Bao Haiming Screenwriter: Li Wei
Winning awards	2002: Golden Rooster Award for Best Movie 2002: Golden Rooster Award for Best director 2002: Golden Rooster Award for Best Actress 2002: Golden Rooster Award for Best Supporting Actress 2003: China Huabiao Film Awards for Best Actress 2003: Best Actress Award at Beijing College Student Film Festival 2003: Hundred Flowers Award for Best Supporting Actress 2003: Golden Phoenix Award by China Film Performance Art Academy
News reports and interviews	Yang Yazhou, 2004 interview: [I like] to look at their life and put it down through my camera, because I can see and feel how they make a living, because I am one of them. Initial thoughts of making the film: triggered by an accidental visit to northwest China during which he was "shocked by the local kids' tough living conditions," but also "moved by their genuine warm attitude" towards him and his crew as outsiders. This experience prompted his decision to make a movie eulogizing the common people – the "small potatoes" – who tried hard to make a living in the "middle of nowhere." Response when asked if he had "over glorified" Teacher Zhang in the film: doesn't an ordinary female like Zhang Meili deserve to be put on the big screen and eulogized? There were so many heroic ordinary people doing marvelous work in their common positions. They were worthy to be understood, respected, remembered, and extoled on the big screen. It seems a shame that so few films focus on these kinds of characters and topics.
Public comments/ responses	Imdb review1: Author: HANSDA SOWVENDRA SHEKHAR (hansdass@sify.com) from India March 29, 2006 I had an opportunity to see this wonderful film at the recently concluded Jamshedpur film festival and I consider myself really lucky for being able to do so. This is one worth-talking-about film. There are certain scenes in this movie that really stand out and are there inside the head even days after having seen this film. The relationship between the two women has been portrayed very beautifully. Zhang's outburst at a Beijing mall is quite powerful and touching. That one scene, perhaps, sums up the spirit of the entire picture – how far could a person could go for the sake of others? The opening sequence is equally engaging. The rugged Chinese landscape makes for a very nice visual experience. The lead actors are awesome. Both Pi Ying and Yuan Quan look very good. However, I should make special mention of this child actor (his screen name is Da He). He'll leave you in splits and, in the climax, in tears.

(*Continued*)

Table 3.7 (Continued)

Film title	*Pretty Big Feet*
Public comments/ responses	I'd like to recommend this film to everyone, whether they're serious cinema afficionados or whatever. Movies like this shouldn't be missed for anything.
	Imdb review2: Author: brainfertilizer from United States October 12, 2005 Great movie. It changed my fiancée's life, gave her a goal in life that we will fulfill together: to move to an impoverished village and teach, hopefully helping reinforce the importance of education.
	Douban: User: Girl from Yuan's family April 13, 2009 I cried like a baby when I was watching this movie. At first I thought I would never go to a place like that and work as a volunteer teacher if I was Ms. Xia, but I changed my mind after I watched the whole film.

After all the data were categorized, decoded, and presented separately for each film, we identified emerging themes such as common actions, behaviors, concerns, issues, and contexts related to the director's or characters' intention to communicate, influence, or lead. We discuss our findings in the following chapter.

Notes

1 Yang, Y. (Director). (2003). *Meili de Dajiao* 美丽的大脚 [Pretty Big Feet] [Film]. Western Film Group, Xi'an Film Studio.
2 Zhou, H. (Director). (2005). *Gao San* 高三 [Senior Year] [Film]. Guangdong 21st Century Publishing Co., Ltd.
3 Zhang, Y. (Director). (1999). *Yige Dou Buneng Shao* 一个都不能少 [Not One Less] [Film]. Columbia Pictures (USA), Guangxi Film Studio (China), Beijing New Screen Film Company, Film Productions Asia.
4 Chen W. (Director). (2007). *Qing Touwo Yipiao* 请投我一票 [Please Vote For Me] [Film]. Steps International.
5 Chen W. (Director). (2012). *Chu Lu* 出路 [Education, Education] [Film]. Steps International, The Why Foundation.
6 He Q. (Director). (1994). *Fenghuang Qin* 凤凰琴 [Country Teachers] [Film]. Tianjin Film Studio, Xiaoxiang Film Studio.
7 Pictures were screenshot from the film *Pretty Big Feet*. Copyright belongs to the film production companies: Western Film Group and Xi'an Film Studio.
8 ibid.
9 ibid.

References

Beyerbach, B. (2005). The social foundations classroom: Themes in sixty years of teachers in film: Fast times, dangerous minds, stand on me. *Educational Studies*, *37*(3), 267–285.

Chen, W. (Director). (2007). Qing Tou Wo Yi Piao 请投我一票 [Please Vote For Me] [Film]. Steps International.

Chen, W. (Director). (2012). Chu Lu 出路 [Education, Education] [Film]. Steps International, The Why Foundation.

Fabe, M. (2004). *Closely watched films: An introduction to the art of narrative film technique*. University of California Press.

Foss, S. K. (2004). Framing the study of visual rhetoric: Toward a transformation of rhetorical theory. In C. Hill and M. Helmers (Eds.), *Defining visual rhetorics* (pp. 303–313). Routledge.

He, Q. (Director). (1994). Fenghuang Qin 凤凰琴 [Country Teachers] [Film]. Tianjin Film Studio, Xiaoxiang Film Studio.

Hill, C. A., & Helmers, M. (Eds.). (2012). *Defining visual rhetorics*. Routledge.

Lasswell, H. D. (1948). The structure and function of communication in society. *The Communication of Ideas*, 37, 215–228.

Neuendorf, K. A. (2002). Defining content analysis. *Content analysis guidebook* (pp. 10–27). Sage.

Zhang, Y. (Director). (1999). Yige Dou Buneng Shao 一个都不能少 [Not One Less] [Film]. Columbia Pictures (USA), Guangxi Film Studio (China), Beijing New Screen Film Company, Film Productions Asia.

Zhou, H. (Director). (2005). Gao San 高三 [Senior Year] [Film]. Guangdong 21st Century Publishing Co., Ltd.

4 Impossible mission IV

To recognize the discursive leadership through movie lens

Much of our interpretation of leadership intent across the films in our study came about through reading cinema-related documents, interviews, containing filmmaker language and meta-language. This chapter presents the results of this content analysis, including brief synopses, emerging leadership themes depicted, symbolic messages and discourses, and social influential narratives. For each film, we will present narratives that attempt to capture (1) characters' actions or intentions engaged in mobilization of collective volition and/or (2) filmmakers' efforts to engage in social influence through their films as discourse.

Pretty Big Feet[1]

As discussed earlier in this study, a process of influence involving the crafting of narratives can be understood in terms of discursive leadership. A film can thus be viewed as a leadership attempt, process, or struggle involving the mobilization of human, fiscal, and social capital toward the construction of a socially influential narrative. The filmmaking process thus begins as an *attempted* leadership process (i.e., Hemphill's framework presented earlier in this book). For this process and its ultimate product to be considered successful or effective as a discursive leadership, artifact requires the construction of persuasive cinematic syntax – the integration of dialog, sounds, and images into persuasive patterns of social meaning.

The desire and capacity to mobilize cinematic resources can be considered catalytic ingredients of a discursive leadership process. This seems evidenced in the remarks of *Pretty Big Feet* director Yang Yazhou, who in a 2004 interview expressed his sharp attention to the lives of China's common people.

> [I like] to look at their life and put it down through my camera, because I can see and feel how they make a living, because I am one of them.
>
> (Wang & Tian, 2004)

DOI: 10.4324/9781032723778-5

Yang goes on to describe how his initial thoughts of making the film were triggered by an accidental visit to northwest China during which he was "shocked by the local kids' tough living conditions," but also "moved by their genuine warm attitude" toward him and his crew as outsiders. This experience prompted his decision to make a movie eulogizing the common people – the "small potatoes" – who tried hard to make a living in the "middle of nowhere" (Wang & Tian, 2004).

Yang's words reflect the initiation of a creative leadership process, an interpretation seemingly reinforced within Yang's response when asked if he had "over glorified" Teacher Zhang in the film – "Doesn't an ordinary female like Zhang Meili deserve to be put on the big screen and eulogized?" Yang added that he always believed there were so many "heroic ordinary people doing marvelous work in their common positions" and that they were "worthy to be understood, respected, remembered, and extoled on the big screen" (International Herald Leader, 2011).

"It seems a shame," he added, "that so few films focus on these kinds of characters and topics" (International Herald Leader, 2011). One may reasonably infer that in attempting to raise respect, remembrance, and glorification of "heroic ordinary people," Yang's intent is to mobilize popular volition toward understanding the need for heroic action, support for such action, and a wave of collective perceptual and cognitive change that might gradually re-frame such action as more normative than heroic.

Leadership themes, literal and explicit

Pretty Big Feet depicts the arduous life of a middle-aged teacher, Zhang Meili, in a rural northwestern village in China. Earlier in her life, her 23-year-old husband had been tried and executed for stealing railroad spikes and causing a train derailment that killed two people. Believing his poor education had caused her husband's fate, Zhang Meili dedicates her life to teaching and gradually establishes the village's only school. After many years, Xia Yu arrives, a young volunteer who offers hope for stability, new knowledge, and opportunity for the local community. After a series of conflicts, quarrels, and misunderstandings, Ms. Xia and Ms. Zhang begin to understand and care for each other. Ms. Xia, nevertheless, decides to return to her husband in Beijing. Despite this loss, Ms. Zhang presses on, teaching and striving to raise local funds to buy a computer for the school. After just limited success, she submits to the sexual advances of *nouveau riche* "Noodle Zhao" in exchange for his agreement to fund the purchase.

Ms. Xia returns to the village with an invitation for Ms. Zhang and her students to visit Beijing, which they happily accept. Their visit to Beijing is marked by two key events. The first occurs when one student brays like a donkey to the delight and ridicule of a local Beijinger. This triggers a tearful, heartfelt admonishment from Ms. Zhang to her students; they must study hard, overcome elitist urban bigotry, and demonstrate their dignity and value to the nation. The second occurs as Ms. Xia introduces Ms. Zhang to businessman, "Boss Zhang," who agrees to invest in her village's main product – potatoes – to support local education. After returning home, however, Ms. Zhang is fatally injured while transporting potatoes. At this point, Ms. Xia decides to stay on as the village's school teacher.

Explicit leadership themes

We use the term "explicit" to describe manifest leadership acts and processes unfolding within a given cinematic narrative; in other words, the leadership efforts displayed by characters within the film. As discussed previously in this study, acts of leadership – or a leadership process – may be viewed as attempted, successful, or effective depending on the degree to which the individual acts or continued processes lead to changes in behavior or the accomplishment of goals. Most often, however, few clear-cut definitions or boundaries exist that help categorize action or process into one specific stage. In other words, a leadership effort may be viewed from all three vantage points depending upon the time, place, and direction of action.

This framework is particularly useful for evaluating the nature and impact of Teacher Zhang Meili. As the story unfolds, we see her individual acts and overall effort evolve in and out of each leadership stage. The following paragraphs discuss key examples of her engagement in this process.

Building a school

Teacher Zhang's leadership attempts and successes are evidenced both visually and through dialog, with the latter serving to summarize action and meaning at key points of the narrative. For example, early in the movie, character "Film" Wang (the local movie projectionist) speaks to his friend:

> Her [Teacher Zhang's] husband broke the law and was executed out of ignorance when her kid was one year old. She brought her kid up all by herself. She taught him characters every day so that he won't follow his dad's track. At first she only taught her own kid, but then she also taught other village kids, and then she started this school. But then her own kid died. We didn't have any schools before she came.
>
> [00:03:25]

Admiration underlies Wang's remark, as it implies that Teacher Zhang (with no beloved connections to the village after her son's death) could have sought a better life in her home town or in a larger city. Wang and, we assume, other villagers note that she did not do so and thereby recognize her responsibility and passion to help other children change their lives.

Acquiring human resources

In addition to Teacher Zhang's effort to establish the school, the arrival of Xia Yu to the village opens a new opportunity for leadership action. Xia Yu's choice to teach in the village does not appear to have been prompted by dedication. Rather, the film constructs her choice as one of running away from her husband and their messy life. Her first weeks in the village are somewhat awkward and clumsy, suggesting her unwillingness to adapt to local physical and social conditions. Teacher Zhang, wishing her to become integrated and engaged in the school and village, goes to great lengths to provide Xia Yu with special comforts and privileges (clean water, children's special songs, taking care of her laundry, etc.). When Xia Yu insists that she cannot tolerate the taste of the local water, Teacher Zhang offers her a cup of orange tea. Zhang begs Xia Yu to stay but can only persuade her to stay a little longer:

> You are the only volunteer teacher to come to our village from a big city. We have expected you for so long, but now you are leaving so suddenly like this? Miss Xia, you must have seen our situation. Our kids almost know nothing. Can't you leave something more for them? Please, I beg you!
> [00:33:54]

Xia Yu does leave, but, as revealed in the previous section, returns to offer Teacher Zhang and her students the chance to visit Beijing.

Acquiring fiscal resources

Before she left the school, and as she came to understand the eagerness of the students to learn, Xia Yu suggested that the school obtain a computer to facilitate student learning. Though Teacher Zhang liked the idea, she knew it would require a huge expenditure. After Teacher Zhang made several visits with village officials, they agreed to provide about one-third the total cost if she could raise the rest from local donations.

> Teacher Zhang, the last time you came to us you said you wanted to buy a computer for the children. Good! It's quite necessary. However, because we are a poor town, you know our budget is small. But we still tried our best to find you three thousand Yuan. And, we will provide the school with a special telecommunications link. That's all we can offer. You need to seek other ways to get the rest.
> [00:48:48]

The above bit of dialog reveals Teacher Zhang's persuasive impact, as 3,000 yuan was a large investment for the small village. It also suggests the daunting challenge remaining, one which Teacher Zhang was willing to accept.

Her success would come at great personal cost. The village's wealthiest businessman, "Noodle" Zhao, was planning a memorial party for his mother. Teacher Zhang saw opportunity and organized her students to sing – persuasively – for the old man.

> Mr. Zhao, you are so lucky, your mom lived to eighty-seven,
> Eighty-seven is a long life, No one in the village has lived so long,
> Everyone in the village is happy for you.
> Mr. Zhao, you are such a dutiful son, as we can tell you are such a good person!
> Mr. Zhao, you are rich, you should make some contribution to local education,
> We just want to buy a computer, Children say please make a contribution to our school,
> Make a contribution! Make a contribution!
> [00:52:04]

But Mr. Zhao is unmoved. He asks Teacher Zhang, "Drink with me tonight," meaning, of course, more than just a drink. Teacher Zhang tries to drink with him there at the party, but Zhao insists on an evening tryst as requirement for any donation. One may conclude that Teacher Zhang's individual leadership attempt has failed with respect to Zhao. Yet, her willingness to sacrifice and even debase herself in exchange for funding can also be viewed as part of a larger leadership struggle.

Building commitment and engagement

Although Xia Yu left the village, she returned with an invitation to Teacher Zhang and her students to tour Beijing. At one point during the trip a seemingly wealthy young man wearing designer sunglasses and expensive clothing pays for the children's entrance to an indoor playground to play with his kid. Laughing when he heard one of the children (Wang Dahe) mimicking a donkey, "Sunglasses" called the boy over to repeat the "heehaw" sound. Witnessing this, Teacher Zhang viewed it as a form of humiliation – innocent poor children being mocked by a wealthy urbanite. She then delivers a heartfelt tearful admonishment to the students.

> Stop! Stop! Wang Dahe, if I hear you do that braying again I will punish you! Is Beijing good? Yes, everything is good in Beijing. What do we have in our village? Go back and study hard, Children! Please study hard so that we don't need to grow potatoes and eat potatoes every day. Otherwise you will never come to anything. We should study hard and enter colleges in Beijing. We will build our village as good as Beijing. Then we won't have

to get a free tour and be pitied and looked down upon for mimicking a donkey as they asked. Aren't you silly and naïve? I didn't pay the entrance fee for you kids and you are tall enough to be charged. Why enter the playground? Kids, I am getting old and I tell you again, you should study hard. You are the only hope of our village. Right? You must study hard so you don't need to make a living growing potatoes. Did you hear me, Dahe? I should not blame you for that. It is me who's not good enough and doesn't have the money to pay. Don't tell Teacher Xia about this. I shouldn't have blamed you. It is just because you still didn't study hard when I told you. Now you see the distance between our life and the city people's life. You have to study hard. There is no other way out, right?

[01:14:41]

A simple reading of the above dialog is insufficient to understand the power of this scene. By the end of Teacher Zhang's appeal Wang Dahe and the other children are crying along with her. It is an extremely moving moment in the film for both the children and the audience.

Thus, within the story of the film, Teacher Zhang brings hope and change to the village. Through continued, persistent actions and efforts (some of which failed in the short run) she is able to garner resources and strengthen educational structures throughout the village. People increasingly paid attention to her mission. We see this last point emphasized at the end of the movie when "Film" Wang projects his beam of light upon the school building as if to honor Teacher Zhang's efforts and impact.

To summarize further, Teacher Zhang acted as an altruistic mother figure in the film. Her dedication and selflessness moved the local citizens, especially the children and others close to her. Her leadership is revealed in her persistence, encouragement, spirit, and results. She expanded her zone of acceptance as others suspended their own judgment in favor of hers. A famous sentence from a classic Chinese poem offers an apt description of Teacher Zhang: 春蚕到死丝方尽,蜡炬成灰泪始干, (chūn cán dào sǐ sī fang jìn, là jù chéng huī lèi shǐ gān), which means a silk worm keeps spinning silk till the end of its life, a candle goes on lighting us till burning itself out. Zhang Meili is a representative of the traditional teacher figure in China, who is willing to dedicate her personal life, all her energy, and her happiness into the career of teaching in the remote little village. However, it might be hard to understand and appreciate from view of the West. Thus, through this film, we can see that to influence others through moving them can be one way of demonstrating leadership in Chinese society.

Patterns of symbolic meaning

A cinematic narrative's persuasive impact is, perhaps, first rooted in an effective translation of tangible resources into literal patterns of meaning.

Characters, events, and dialog representing ideas, beliefs, and values are thus woven into what may justly be called "an argument." The argument consists of literal and implicit components. The literal components of *Pretty Big Feet* have already been discussed. We now shift to the film's symbolic component, which consists largely of visual imagery. Symbols and their meanings often flow from filmmaker intent but may also be independently constructed by individual viewers (a perspective from critical literary theory) (Boggs, 1996). Filmmakers use symbols to focus upon and reinforce attention to particular patterns of meaning. Viewers (again from the critical perspective) may discern additional implicit themes that relate to, push beyond, or conflict with the film's explicit argument. Throughout the movie, director Yang appears to have intended his audiences to notice various symbolic messages. These are the focus of the following sections.

Water/Rain

When asked about his initial thoughts on making *Pretty Big Feet*, director Yang stressed how the severe water shortage in the small northwestern China village intrigued his interest (Wang & Tian, 2004). Water, and the lack of it, is a key theme throughout the movie. Water is the source of life and something that most people in China today can take for granted. But in Teacher Zhang's village, which has received no significant rain for more than three years, water is precious.

Water and rain repeatedly appear in the film as symbols of resource inequality. In one later scene, for example, the village students are startled when they see a large pool of water in a bath center in Beijing. One child, Wang Dahe, is shocked to the point that he pees in his bathrobe. By the time this scene appears, rain and water have already repeatedly appeared as tools of greater meaning. For example, the village's need for rain and water parallels its need for education and economic development. The first image of this is found in the volunteer teacher's name, Xia Yu, which in Mandarin is pronounced the same as "falling rain." Xia Yu's arrival means hope for a better quality life of the local people, like a timely rain poured on arid land.

As the movie continues, the symbolic meaning of rain and water morphs into something different; the eagerness – and also the hopelessness of the local people. The theme is artfully phrased within the subplot involving Xia Yu's decision to return to Beijing after having contributed only modestly toward Teacher Zhang's goals. Despite the villagers' wish for she to stay, Xia Yu "can't drink the local water." Her temporary presence seemed insufficient and unsatisfying, like "thunder without rain."

The idea of thunder without rain is previously introduced in an earlier scene [01:05:26–01:06:38]. It is a typical afternoon and students are reading a lesson called "Thunder Rain." The students copy quietly as Ms. Xia writes new words on the chalkboard. A series of loud thunder crashes break the quiet air – the children rush outside. The director's use of two medium close-up shots (MCU) capturing Xia Yu and Zhang Meili's reactions and expressions along with many kids running in front of them generates a tense uncertainty for viewers. The camera follows the group outside. In a manner that first appears haphazard, the children and their teachers run to fetch any sort of containers they can find. Objects fall from shelves and shatter on the ground. Children trip and fall. But within a minute, they are all standing still, holding their containers, and waiting silently for rain.

After a longshot "bird's eye view" of the crowd and various containers, the camera turns to a medium shot of the sun, followed by several high-angle medium shots revealing a gradually frustrated expression of the teachers and some of their students. The camera returns to the sun and the scene gradually fades.

Within this scene, the extremely high camera angle longshot and the stillness of the crowd reveal the helpless and desperate feeling of the crowd. By putting the audience in a godlike position, looking down on the action, director Yang presses the segment's initial hope and ultimate disappointment into audience perception. Despite the dearth of rain and water, however, subsequent scenes reveal how villagers allow teachers to fetch water from public reservoirs first, without waiting in line, as a way of showing respect for the value of education. If we say water is the source of life, then through the movie we can perceive a message that education is the source of a better life.

Big feet

As the title of the movie suggests, Zhang Meili's big feet symbolize her personality, worldview, and life story. The movie begins, in fact, with a close-up shot on Zhang Meili's big feet walking fast accompanied by a shift from the black-and-white past to colorful present and ends with another close-up shot on Zhang Meili's big feet in stillness, indicating her death.

Until relatively recently, small feet were highly valued and admired in Chinese society. Young girls were compelled to have their feet bound from early childhood to keep them looking small and eventually attract a good husband. For centuries, women's natural "big feet" were considered ugly and associated with provincial people and rustic life. Even as time went by, people, especially uneducated people in rural areas, still held the belief that a woman with "big feet" was unattractive and unmarriageable. Thus, by picking this name, director challenges the traditional social norm.

With her big feet, Teacher Zhang represented rural women of the new era who fight against such repressive norms. But while she feels ashamed and unsuccessful for having "a pair of ugly big feet," she follows her heart's desire against all obstacles in her way. As a teacher, Zhang Meili started her own school out of a wish that kids would lead a better life through education. She dedicated almost her entire life to her teaching career and never complained a word.

Clean and dirty

Contrasting details suggest a message that sometimes affluent people with clean appearances may have polluted souls – "Noodle Zhao," for instance. In contrast, poor people might look dirty or untidy but have soft and genuine hearts. This is taking aim at the idea that it is wrong to judge people by their appearance, or to imagine "wealth" to represent status or hard work. Poor people from rural village who worked hard to make a living deserve more respect and a helping hand from society.

Xia Yu serves as a vehicle for this message, as the film presents an obvious transition in her appearance. Upon her arrival in the village, she dresses in black outfits with her face completely covered by a black scarf, black hat, and black sunglass, ostensibly as a barrier to the sand and dirt floating in the air. Her expression is difficult to recognize behind the shield. Xia Yu even hesitates momentarily when offered "clean" water for washing her face, put off by its cloudy appearance. When Wang Dahe first greets Xia Yu, he takes the can of Coke (perhaps an uncommon item in the village) and runs down the sandy hill, prompting Xia to cover her face to block the dusty sands and dirt he kicks up. When she puts her hands down, Xia's face is mixed with shock, sadness, and confusion – apparently uncomfortable being so close to the "earthy" village. Yet at the end of the movie, after Zhang's death, Xia Yu returns to the sandy hill. After a deep breath, she jumps and slides down with a resolute and composed face. The sand and dirt on face no longer matter. She has transformed from a self-centered woman who cared about appearances to a thoughtful, kind, and cheerful giver who seems comfortable with the village and its earthiness. Her heart and soul shine as her face is covered with village dust.

All these signals make us wonder. Does our wealth and cleanliness make it rarer and more difficult for us to share with others? In the early 1960s, most all of China was still very poor with most of its citizens living in rural areas and working on farms. People would share dinner with their neighbors and look out for each other. With wealth and urban migration, however, the distance between people seemed to grow. Have people become colder and more detached? More selfish, defensive, and judgmental to one another? Does abundance threaten trust, kindness, and the sense of generosity to those in need? Do clean and pretty appearances hide selfishness and indifference? Director Yang seems to pose these questions in *Pretty Big Feet* and in so doing challenges his audience to consider if whatever debt they may owe their hard-working rural brothers and sisters might be at least partially paid by increasing educational equity.

Sunglasses and leather jacket

"Sunglasses" and "leather jacket" appear as stereotypes held by many of China's rural citizens toward affluent urbanites – Teacher Zhang several times warns her students to keep away from those who sport them.

Villagers apparently also pre-judge people by their appearance, and sunglasses/leather jackets appear as another theme representing mistrust and misunderstanding. Director Yang reinforces the point of how appearances and façades lead us to forget our most important asset, social assets.

Senior Year

Senior Year did not get much attention from the public when it was first shown on China Central Television (CCTV) in 2005, but one year later, after receiving several national awards, it gradually attracted attention and provoked tremendous response and discussion across China. *Senior Year* loosely follows a student's (Lin Jiayan) diary to push the storyline and timeline forward. Director Zhou Hao filmed the normal daily life of the students in Grade 12, Class 7, Wuping No.1 High School, for many years one of the best high schools in Fujian province.

Director Zhou's initial thought of making this documentary grew after viewing the documentary, *Secondary School*, filmed and directed by Zhang Hong in Hong Kong in 2002 (Liu, 2007). According to director Zhou, he didn't plan to make the National College Entrance Exam (NCEE) the main focus of the film. Instead, he simply wanted to "capture the growing process of an ordinary teenage kid from an average county in China" (Southern Metropolis Daily, 2006). The film nevertheless turned out to be a remarkable and influential portrayal of how Chinese youth prepare for the NCEE (Wang, 2006).

The film highlights, at times (at least for non-Chinese viewers) almost painfully, the collective ordeal facing Chinese 12th-grade students, whose lives will be forever affected by the results of the NCEE. For Chinese viewers, the film may be viewed in numerous ways ranging from a bit of warm nostalgia to a stunning examination of the "education fever" problem built into the structure of Chinese education. Some viewers may see it as an invitation to consider the possibility of more humane educational alternatives (Southern Metropolis Daily, 2006).

The power of documentary

Throughout years of Chinese cinema, the documentary has been used primarily as an educational tool, but mostly to present "official" knowledge to Chinese viewers (Mao, 2011). Over the past 30 years, however, Chinese directors began to utilize their greater freedom to draw public attention to areas of social concern. Thus, in contrast to the "official knowledge" style, the documentary film took a more "folktale" style, with directors finding ways to create new narratives of social understanding (Mao, 2011). Though no longer limited to the presentation of official persuasion or directive, the documentary remained a powerful tool for shaping public attention, concern, and discussion.

Director Zhou Hao, known as "Master Zhou" among his former colleagues and friends, was a former professional press photographer in China's Xinhua News Agency of China. In 2000, Zhou made up his mind to give up his steady and promising position to work for "China's most influential liberal newspaper" (Rosenthal, 2002), *Southern Weekend*. In his new position, Zhou won photography awards throughout the world for his unique focus upon the interaction between man and environment (Liu, 2007). As time passed, however, his "strong desire for storytelling" could no longer be satisfied by still camera alone.

> [I like] to communicate with the world by making documentaries. I have the freedom to say anything I want [through documentaries]. There are no restrictions. I couldn't find a more suitable way to express [my thoughts].
> (Lin, 2013)

From a photographer to documentary film director, what remains the same is Zhou Hao's strong enthusiasm for recording personally and socially important and influential ideas and stories. With that in mind, it is no great leap to infer that *Senior Year* was intended to record a common "state of mind" that would resonate with those who had experienced a "senior year" as well as those who had not (Chen, 2006). The importance of this type of communication through film was stressed by director Zhou during one interview.

> I don't want my films to remain aloof from the world. I want to see [my documentaries] strike a responsive chord in the hearts of the audience. I enjoy applause.
> (Liu, 2007)

Zhou Hao goes on to note that since the restoration of NCEE in 1977, the whole society has been "affected by the event," as it has deeply influenced life of "thousands of students and their families" for an entire year. It would be "a shame," he continued, if no one captured the experience on film. Moreover, he suggested that if more and more independent film directors would demonstrate a "unique way of looking at things" to the public, it might gradually "break [society's] predominant centralized perception" of the event. Thus, one key potential function of documentary filmmaking is to "pay attention" to the "social public space" (Liu, 2007).

Discursive leadership

Due to the significant influence of NCEE on thousands of students and their families, the high school senior year (*gaosan*) has attracted increasing social attention, especially for those at the lower middle or bottom class of the society.

To most Chinese parents and students, getting a high NCEE score and entering a four-year university is a "turning point" in their lives. It also represents, by any practical standard, "the only way" to get out of small villages and live a better life. In *Senior Year*, director Zhou depicts the situation by aiming his lens not only at students and parents, but primarily at head teacher Wang. A dynamic teacher, Wang, asks his students to give up "half of their life" and to eat "bitterness" during their senior year to prepare for the NCEE. One of the students' mother expresses her hope to her daughter that "you should study hard and get into the university, so that you can live a better life, a much better life than us." Another student's father declares directly to the camera that being a peasant means endless hard work and low social status, a path he does not want his daughter to follow.

Especially after receiving the Humanitarian Award for Documentaries at the 30th Hong Kong International Film Festival in 2006, *Senior Year* has become more influential within social discourse. Multiple and diverse responses and interpretations have emerged, many of which fell completely out of director Zhou's anticipation.

> After the film [Senior Year] was released, one response was that I made an inspiring film. At the moment, I was not so happy with the response, for I don't see how it would inspire people. But gradually I understand that different people might have different insights towards the same movie, which is quite normal and actually quite good.
>
> (Liu, 2007)

When asked about what motivated him for this particular film, director Zhou answered in an artfully way,

> To put it simple, I see my film as a mirror – that would reflect what we look like to those who seldom take a look at themselves. And which would make them pause and think. That's pretty enough.
>
> (Liu, 2007)

These insights offered by director Zhou seem to run parallel with and prompt consideration of some key concepts in Western organization theory; specifically, distributed decision-making and transformational leadership. Consider, for example, how a transformational school principal faced with pressures for curricular reform might pose a series of questions to his or her faculty, encourage responses, encounter unexpected responses, and finally whittle down the question to something like, "what kind of school do we want to become"?

Moreover, similar to what the above school principal might hope for, Zhou added (Liu, 2007) that he wished his film generated would gradually "get more people involved" in the topic of NCEE, thereby leading to a more comprehensive form of social/public understanding. This constitutes director

Zhou's attempt to lead others through the use of his film as a stimulant to motivate citizens to pay attention to an issue he considers critical. As he stressed,

> I don't expect my film would have any influence on the NCEE system, but at least it can work as a good cause for people to refocus on this issue. I hope eventually [people's concern] will make the NCEE system better.
>
> (Liu, 2007)

Coincidentally or as a result, the structure of NCEE has been slightly revised year-by-year and place-by-place. For example, many provinces and cities have recently gained the right to design their own college entrance exam test topics for their students.

Whether viewed as an inspirational tribute to academic diligence or as a critical question mark aimed at a system's brutal intensity, *Senior Year* compels Chinese society to set their eyes – again and with less nostalgia – on the NCEE's impact on student life. Questions that may thus emerge include, "how are students' lives proceeding after enduring the *Gaosan* ordeal?" "Do those who do well, who enter their 'dream university,' experience substantial change in their life, happiness, and social status?" "And, do those with unsatisfactory scores on the NCEE become locked forever into their small village lives?"

Some such questions were addressed by a subsequent 90-minute television broadcast in which Teacher Wang and several of his students were asked to reflect on their lives after high school graduation from Wuping No. 1 High School. Notwithstanding the comments of Wang or his students, the broadcast suggests the discursive social wave that swelled up in the months after *Senior Year*'s release.

The wave is further evidenced by the increasing number of documentaries focusing on different high schools and their preparation for NCEE. For instance, in 2008, British Broadcasting Corporation (BBC) put on a series of documentaries named *Chinese School*, which included five episodes focused on the lives of a group of families, teachers and children during the course of a single academic year in the rural town of Xiu Ning in Anhui province. In the same year, America's Public Broadcasting Service (PBS) telecasted a documentary, *China Prep*, following five Chinese students through their senior year and revealing their preparation and fierce competition at an elite high school in Sichuan Province. Later in 2011, director Wang Yang produced a documentary called *China Gate* about how students and their whole families living in West China's Hui Ning poverty-stricken (but known for producing top scholars) county prepared for NCEE exams.

Thus, although some of the reactions and responses about the film turned out to be unexpected to director Zhou, *Senior Year* may be thought of as a successful act of discursive leadership, as it led enduring attention to a key public issue and pointed a direction for further observation and investigation. Sometimes, to lead means to provide a different way of thinking, a different angle of looking at thing, or a fresh opportunity for reflection.

Explicit leadership portrayal within the film[2]

In terms of explicit leadership action, the spotlight falls on Wang Jianchun, the head teacher of students in Grade 12 and Class 7. Teacher Wang is a dedicated, motivated, and encouraging leader of the students and their parents in what he refers to as the "battle of life." He dedicates nearly all his waking time and energy to his students, knows them well, and displays consistent empathy. Teacher Wang is presented as knowing when to push his students hard, when to soothe their nerves, and how to communicate with students at different levels of ability and motivation. Director Zhou stated in tongue-in-cheek fashion that Teacher Wang "is such a good teacher, it makes me feel so sorry that I didn't run into him when I was in school. Otherwise, I might be doing even better now" (Liu, 2007).

The documentary technique employed by director Zhou greatly resembles that often seen on Western-style "reality television," a style that should resonate with anyone who has ever watched an episode of *Ramsey's Kitchen Nightmares*. Throughout the film, Teacher Wang is shown giving a "full Ramsey treatment" to his students. The film begins, for example, with a flash-back scene of him shouting at two students in the early morning in their dormitory for having fallen asleep during exams and being late for class. Teacher Wang seems so irritated and full of anger. He loses his temper, swears that the boys are "hopeless," and wonders aloud why they even "bother come to school." After getting the two out of bed, Wang paces back and forth in the school courtyard, cigarette in his hand to calm him down. He points toward the classroom and sighs worriedly that he "couldn't change their behavior no matter by stick or carrot." He then gazes off, as if deep in thought. At this point, one might assume Wang to be merely a foul-tempered coach, an assumption belied throughout the rest of the film.

In fact, Teacher Wang is later seen acting as both father and coach to his students. In "good cop – bad cop" style, he shows caring for all of them, and spends much time with students who appear to be falling behind. When necessary, he gives the "falling behind" students some realistic suggestions for their future. Although students are discouraged or prohibited from spending much evening time in the city (this is a boarding school), he promises two internet-addicted students time off on Saturday nights to persuade them to persist in studying. He engages deeply with one rebellious student to behave himself to avoid being expelled. After a round of tough talk, he calms and encourages the downbeat, fearful, self-abased, depressed, and frustrated students with consoling words.

Teacher Wang uses different communicate approaches toward female and male students. For female students he tends to use comforting words, joking tones, soft warnings, and encouraging patting on the back. With male students, his words tend to be louder, more straight-forward, and focused on tough requirements. Body language and contact include pats on the back and arms over the shoulder. After the hard-edged opening scene, director Zhou's camera captures the fullness of this coach-teacher; his dedication, reliability, energy, and authentic concern.

An American friend who watched the film considered Teacher Wang as a tough, vigorous football coach or drill sergeant, whose authority is well understood and virtually unquestioned by the students entering his classroom. The events captured by the camera suggest that, as with a coach or drill sergeant, Wang's reputation has preceded him. We see the opening day of the school year, when Wang begins by telling the class, "This will be your toughest year.... I will treat you strictly, for your own good!"

Wang's next moves aim at building confidence through reasoning and discipline. Citing classic Chinese poetry, he continues,

> Now we know what our goal is. And we have confidence (to achieve it). The next step is how to take action. Scholar Wang Guowei divided life into three phases. The first one we mentioned earlier.
> Westerly winds withered trees last night,
> Climbing up the stairs alone
> I overlooked the endless distance.

This is a process of encouraging and consolidating yourselves. Next comes

> Languishing in missing you
> I have no regrets becoming emaciated for you."

Now you've set up your goal and confidence, then it's time to take actions. Take actions! So, I tell you, in your senior year, you must be prepare to eat bitterness. Every year, I would ask my senior year students to give me half of your life [class chuckles]. Just half of your life. I don't want your whole life. Because as far as I know, nobody has ever died or fainted in the classroom from studying too hard [whole class laughs]. You are no exceptions. You must go through it. So I hope you can eat the bitterness. And don't feel bad about me when I am strict to you, for I do that in the best interest of you. To put it in popular words, "I love you anyway."

[00:06:23–00:08:20]

Encouraging, even virtually forcing the students to work hard in their last year, Wang later meets with parents to clarify the situation and garner their unconditional support. He emphatically reminds parents of the importance of

NCEE and asks them to form a "harmonious environment" during the senior year for the best interest of the kids. To quote Teacher Wang,

> In this year, I hope all the parents can create a harmonious family atmosphere. Don't consider anything like divorce, even if you want to, wait until your kids pass the NCEE.
>
> [00:10:34–00:10:51]

After the parent meeting, Wang meets parents one by one to review their child's prior test results and explain their current overall position. Based on his knowledge of each student, he suggests different coping approaches to the parents. "Do your job! Pay more attention to her personal life! I will do the rest!" Wang treats parents respectfully but, in a very real sense, also like "support staff," who ought not to put up any barrier to his strong leadership style.

Gradually, Teacher Wang uses various persuasive tools on his students – inspiring songs, poetry, and slogans. He even offers at one point to "take the blame and resign" for their disappointing test scores. Another teacher's class had done better overall, and so he stressed his sense of feeling "looked down upon" by that teacher. "But now we can have a fresh start and beat them on the NCEE!" As he speaks, the camera traces every student's face, showing them frowning, yet listening carefully with their eyes still gazing at the textbooks.

To enhance students' collective morale and sense of group honor, Teacher Wang encourages them to speak out their thoughts and opinions at regular class meetings. Zhong Shengming, a student who might be considered "bad" for often skipping classes and breaking school rules, gives a powerful speech during this class meeting, saying,

> A dragon has nine children, and each of them is different. There are good students, average students, and poor students. I think if poor students like me, who are still wavering and feel lost, can keep chin up and never give up, then there a famous quote for us, "there must come a time when we will be successful and respected by all."
>
> [00:25:30–00:26:08]

His distinctive and powerful words seem to inspire his classmates and prompt a burst of applause. As we can see, gradually, students in this documentary, like comrades in the same battle, are tightly bonded with each other. And they strive to lead one another – an additional lesson embedded within Wang's strategy.

> Years later, we might be in different places around the world saying with one voice, "I am proud to be a graduate of Class 7 Grade 12 in Wuping No.1 High School." And make yourself a legend!
>
> [00:26:09–00:26:41]

They comfort each other by sharing their feelings and dreams. They support and keep an eye on each other. Although they need to compete with each other on the NCEE test, they still support each other to walk through the toughest period, the senior year, together. Teacher Wang epitomizes the essential definition of leadership – he mobilizes popular volition.

Teacher Wang's concern may be test scores, but his students are more than numbers. The film presents examples in which Wang approaches students who he thinks may be in a difficult position and in need of guidance. He relaxes the nervous ones with warm and funny words. He soothes the sad ones with inspiring and meaningful conversations. He speaks reason to the misbehaving ones. When Wang finds out one of his students, Zhang Xingwang, has an emotional breakdown and tried to run away from the coming NCEE tests in 14 days, he rushes to the bus station to find him store by store. After discovering Xingwang at a restaurant, he has a long conversation with him and successfully changes his mind and has him promise to endure the last few days and take the NCEE no matter what the result might be. Wang is presented as both taskmaster and father figure – a powerful blend of two key leader dimensions.

As time goes by, we can see that under Teacher Wang's continuous construction of communication, mutual understanding, and trust, his bonds with students become tighter and stronger, even for the most rebellious student, Ming. Although Ming has been dressed down by Teacher Wang so many times, he holds no grudges. Instead, after getting a "warning" for breaking school regulations, he feels sorry and wants to apologize to Teacher Wang out of his fear that what he did might cause the teacher trouble. There is a unique commitment between students and their teacher. In the senior year, Wang strives to help his students feel secure and confident. He becomes their rock.

At the end of the film, when the NCEE finally comes, Wang stands on a table to address his class. The camera presents him as a commander addressing his troops prior to battle, offering last-minute heart-stirring encouragements to boost their courage before they walk into the examination room,

> Persistence is the secret of victory! We already overcame so many difficulties. And now it's time for the final "attack." The full surge has begun. And I look forward for your triumph! I wish each of our classmates success! One, two, three, say "we made it!" We made it! [said by all students in unison with smiles on their faces.]
>
> [01:28:16–01:28:38]

The film ends with Teacher Wang introducing himself to another class of senior year students as their head teacher. In this very first meeting, he shares a poem to signify the starting point of a new cycle of battlement,

> I wouldn't care, success or failure, for I will only struggle ahead as long as I have been destined, to the distance.
>
> [01:33:26–01:33:33]

As we can see, in the NCEE battle, Teacher Wang is the commander and leader that needs to boost morale and give directions to different soldiers every year to make sure together all of them would at least survive the fight.

It's true that many people throughout the world know something about the rigorous nature of Chinese high schools. But knowing about it, thinking about it, and acting about it are entirely different components of a developing social mindset. Director Zhou's work reminds audiences of this as it presses us along this emotional and intellectual path.

Not One Less

Not One Less (Yige Dou Buneng Shao) tells a story set in a small rural Chinese village whose only primary school teacher, Gao Enman, must leave for one month to care for an elderly parent. The village mayor can find no one to take his place other than an awkward 13-year-old girl, Wei Minzhi, whose primary motivation appears to be the small money she will earn for serving as a substitute. Before he leaves, Gao tries to explain as much as he can to an obviously inept Minzhi about teaching. A major concern for Gao is the possibility that some of the poor students will drop out while he's gone because their families are in dire need of the income that they could earn by seeking work. He tells Minzhi he will add 10 yuan to her pay if all the students are still in school when he returns.

So when one of the boys, Zhang Huike, leaves for the nearby city to search for a job, Wei Minzhi, mostly out of fear of losing money, plots to go find him and bring him back. Wei Minzhi and her students muddle through a series of failed efforts to raise money for a bus ticket, until out of sheer frustration she simply begins walking the ridiculously long distance toward the city. After hours of fruitless walking, she is offered a ride by some workers on a flatbed truck. Once she arrives in the city, it becomes apparent – again – that her strategies to find Zhang have little chance of succeeding. And yet, partly due to Wei Minzhi's "ignorant persistence" (Kraicer, 2001; Zhang, 2001), but mostly due to the kindness of a few strangers, Zhang is found. During the entire process, Wei Minzhi's motivation for finding him gradually changes from financial interest to a genuine concern for the wellbeing of her student. On the surface, the film has an uplifting finish. The city's television station turns the story of Wei Minzhi and Zhang Huike into a piece of public interest "infotainment." The two children are returned to their village school as heroes, along with cash and supplies raised through the TV station's appeal to viewers.

Not One Less as discursive leadership

In terms of how it has been defined in this study, "leadership" is mostly absent in the narrative presented by *Not One Less*. Although the film is often presented and perceived as a heartwarming story of a young girl's persistence in the face of great odds, with few exceptions, the motivations and actions of its characters range from selfish indifference to helpless sympathy. *Not One Less* thus presents a complex challenge for those seeking to frame it in the context of "educational leadership." The key to this challenge is to first accept the characters for the authentic, non-heroic, and often obtuse individuals that they are. Once this is done, the film's underlying discursive message appears not only powerful in terms of educational leadership but also somewhat troubling from a sociological perspective.

The intention of the director

In 1999, director Zhang Yimou presented two movies, *Not One Less* and *The Road Home*, both of which focused on rural people's lives and challenges. The two films caused an incident at the Cannes Film Festival that year when the festival's committee chair suggested that because *Not One Less* looked like a political propaganda product, Zhang Yimou should only submit *The Road Home* to run for the competition. Angered, Zhang Yimou withdrew both films in protest and claimed they were both apolitical. In an open letter published in the Beijing Youth Daily Zhang accused the festival of being motivated by other than artistic concerns. Zhang wrote,

> What I can't accept is that it seems there's only one way to interpret Chinese film for the westerners – the political way of interpretation. Based on their judgment, Chinese films are either "anti-government" or "political propaganda." It is so naïve and biased to judge a movie based on simple ideas like that.
>
> (Zhang, 1999)

Zhang viewed the problem as a form of prejudice, as "discrimination against Chinese films" (Zhang, 1999). He then sent *Not One Less* to the Venice Film Festival and won the Golden Lion award. In an interview for the Venice festival, Zhang explained his previous action, saying that while political influence on film production in China is unavoidable, cultural differences lead Westerners to view all Chinese film from a political angle (Kraicer, 2001). He also stressed that withdrawing the two films from Cannes Film Festival was "a way to express my attitude and send a message to the public" (Kraicer, 2001). When asked about his intention by making a film like this, director Zhang revealed his disposition toward using films as a vehicle for public influence stating,

> Indeed, no matter the content of the story, the way of telling the story is quite plain and traditional. You can say Not One Less is a "cliché" movie. But that is one of our intentions – to show the reality and power through a common occurrence. As a movie maker these days, we want to produce interesting and eye-catching movies. However, another intention of mine

is to show the audience things and people that they might not aware of, think of, and care for. And I believe that the audience zone of acceptance is not so limited and small as we assumed.

(Kraicer, 2001)

Clearly, Zhang intended Not One Less to have some social influence. The question then remains, what was his message?

The critical discourse of Not One Less

Perhaps the most curious characteristic of *Not One Less* is its pseudo-documentary approach. The storyline, though fictional, presents a problem pervasive to rural Chinese. That is, poor citizens have limited access to only the most rudimentary schooling and strong pressures for students to leave school to go to work. The large cast consists solely of amateur actors whose real names and occupations resemble those of the characters they play in the film – "people playing variations of themselves in front of the camera" (Rea, 2000). For instance, deputy TV station manager Wu Wanlu plays a TV station manager in the film. The main actors, Wei Minzhi and Zhang Huike, were selected from a pool of thousands of poor rural students (Kraicer, 2001). (The names and occupations of the film's main actors are listed in Table 4.1.)

Table 4.1 Not One Less, Character/Actor Matches

Character	Name	Actor's occupation
Teacher Wei Minzhi	Wei Minzhi	Middle school student
Student Zhang Huike	Zhang Huike	Primary school student
Mayor Tian	Tian Zhenda	Mayor of a village in Yanqing County
Teacher Gao	Gao Enman	Village teacher in Yanqing County
Sun Zhimei, who helps Wei search for Zhang Huike in the city	Sun Zhimei	Middle school student
TV station receptionist	Feng Yuying	Ticket clerk
TV show host	Li Fanfan	TV show host
Sports recruiter	Zhang Yichang	Sports instructor
Brickyard owner	Xu Zhanqing	Mayor of a village in Yanqing County
Zhang Huike's sick mother	Liu Hanzhi	Villager
Man in bus station	Ma Guolin	Clerk
TV station manager	Wu Wanlu	Deputy manager of a broadcasting station
Train station announcer	Liu Ru	Announcer for a broadcasting station
Stationery store clerk	Wang Shulan	Stationery store manager
TV show director	Fu Xinmin	TV station head of programming
Restaurant owner	Bai Mei	Restaurant manager

Zhang's stated intent was to "restore the story in a realistic and authentic way" (Kraicer, 2001). More than that, however, Zhang's purpose appears to be to blur or erase what amounts to an artificial distinction between documentary and fictional film; to force viewers to recognize the reality behind the folk tale narrative he presents. In a nutshell (one to be cracked open in the following section), far from being a story about hope and the power to succeed through rugged determination, *Not One Less* is a story of helplessness and futility among the poor, its message suggesting that the poor will never advance their social status without proactive assistance from their more fortunate fellow citizens.

Although both films carry themes of rugged determination in a rural educational setting, the message of *Not One Less* sharply contrasts that of *Pretty Big Feet*, which presents the almost flawless, considerate, and dedicated teacher Zhang Meili who is willing to dedicate her entire life to the kids out of pure concern and love. She is the inspirational hero who can overcome most obstacles to create a "dreamland" of hope with the help of her super progeny, Xia Yu. The message is clear: we need more heroes, and those heroes need our support. But if *Pretty Big Feet*'s Teacher Zhang is a cinematic hero, *Not One Less*'s Teacher Wei is an antihero, the individual who repeatedly struggles and fails, yet who is ultimately saved by the attention of sympathetic observers.

At the outset of *Not One Less*, it is clear that Wei is a reluctant substitute. She barely remembers any of her own third-grade lessons. She can sing only one song. She fails to take the slightest steps to organize a classroom. Her actions explicitly indicate her primary desire to be that of obtaining her salary and promised bonus for preventing any student from dropping out.

> Wei Minzhi, you look after the students. More than ten have already left. I don't want to lose any more. The mayor promised fifty yuan; he'll make sure you get it. If all the students are here when I get back – not one less – you'll get an extra ten yuan. – Teacher Gao, Not One Less.
> [11:08–11:27]

Limited by her age, experience, and apathy, Wei Minzhi displays neither teaching skill nor authority and she doesn't appear to care. She simply copies text onto the blackboard, expecting that students will copy it in their notebooks. When they protest, she sits outside with her back against the door, shutting the students in while she shuts herself out. Wei is more like a copy machine and gatekeeper. She seems incapable of communicating with the students and ultimately can't control them.

As might be the case for most young people her age, she is unable to sort out nuanced situations, for example, not distinguishing between a student dropping out of school and one who is selected by state recruiters to attend a special school for talented athletes. Fearing she will lose her bonus, Wei Minzhi tries to hide the athletically talented student away from her potential opportunity at a better school.

After her one student, Zhang Huike, actually does drop out, Wei Minzhi's poor arithmetic ability foils her best plan for traveling to the city to return him home. After eventually reaching the city (almost by accident), she seems totally unable to understand or cope with the problems involved in finding a wandering nine-year-old boy in a large Chinese city. Only a few of the many people she meets offer her any constructive help at all. Some of those from whom she seeks help offer only disdain. Having gone without food for 24 hours, and unable to reach anyone of authority inside the city TV broadcast center, Wei Minzhi essentially lies down at its front gate as if to die. Her efforts have been tireless, but ultimately foolish and futile. Her salvation comes out of the luck that the TV station manager, seeing her physical plight, invites her in to talk.

Indeed, her luck has changed. But even when she is put in front of a TV camera to appeal to Zhang Huike, she becomes nervously speechless. But just as her luck seems about to run out, a woman who had given Zhang a menial café job hears the boy's name on TV. Zhang is summoned and then sees Wei Minzhi. The two are united electronically through fate and the modest good will of a few city people. Director Zhang almost seems to be hitting viewers over the head with his message. "Don't you get it? Without your help, these people simply lack the capacity to develop or even survive!"

We next see trucks full of supplies accompanied by a TV news team driving back to the village. Now director Zhang hits us with another point to consider. Zhang Huike is asked by a journalist what he learned in the city, to which he replies, "How it felt to be hungry." Viewers are left to infer that as Zhang began to feel the pain of hunger, so did Wei Minzhi; and we now note that her concern for Zhang Huike has become one of unselfish authentic affiliation.

To summarize, if the image of Zhang Meili stands for the rural teacher's heroic image in Chinese society, then Wei Minzhi represents more of a wake-up call to the public. Both *Pretty Big Feet* and *Not One Less* call upon viewers to lend a hand, but the latter's message now seems much more dire. Rural heroes may be quite rare or, more likely, absent altogether. It may, in fact, be unreasonable to expect poor rural people to better themselves. It is therefore your (the viewers') responsibility and obligation to provide spiritual and economic support so that they may live a more humane and productive life. Director Zhang might also want viewers to notice how much information, resources, tools, and knowledge these poor village people lack. They may seem unlovable for their stubbornness and ignorance, but they are still a part of the society that should not be left behind. A hero like Zhang Meili is honorable and worthy of applause and imitation. Yet, what do we do for those such as Wei Minzhi?

The power of mass media

In *Not One Less*, all problems are eventually solved through the institution of television, as if director Zhang's intent is to emphasize the importance and power of mass media in society. The combination of image, sound, and story successfully sends out Wei Minzhi's voice to an audience consisting of intentional news watchers as well as passive viewers who might happen to be viewing in a café or other public place (e.g., Zhang Kehui and the restaurant owner watching over him). At the time of the film's release in 1999, television was the most influential and powerful media throughout China (e.g., cellular phones were not yet the pervasive tool they are today). The TV station plays a critical role in this film as a bridge to connect life between city and village people. Through the camera, poor people can be heard (albeit in a rather haphazard fashion) and receive aid from more affluent viewers. In parallel sense, director Zhang uses *Not One Less* as a powerful tool for raising the problem of – to put it bluntly – rural poverty and ignorance and for reaching out to a nation of otherwise apathetic viewers. In sum, *Not One Less* represents an act of discursive leadership – the creation of a folk tale narrative aimed at generating a social movement.

SOCIAL IMPACT OF NOT ONE LESS

Not One Less caused a great sensation throughout China. Many schools and institutions organized viewings of the film for their leaders, party members, employees, teachers, and students. The film appears to have been manifestly successful in calling people's attention to rural education issues. Many showed an interest in giving a donation to kids in rural areas and some asked about the possibility to help out as a volunteer teacher. Director Zhang's "effective" leadership is also evidenced by the emergence of various Chinese and Western-based organized efforts to mobilize volunteers to visit and assist rural Chinese schools, which we will address in the later paragraphs.

Not One Less also made a sociolinguistic contribution to Chinese society. That is, as the film grew in popularity, its name, "Not One Less (一个都不能少 Yí ge dōu bù néng shǎo)," gradually became a popular phrase used to refer to things related to rural education. For instance, many fundraising activities for rural kids are referred to as a "not one less" activity (Shi, 2000). Other fundraising activities also enlisted the phrase to publicize and mobilize sympathy for Wenchuan earthquake victims. Moreover, even Li Keqiang, the Premier State Council, expressed his concern and encouragement during his visit to a rural northwestern China public school by saying "it is important to make sure every student would benefit from compulsory education, not one less" (Jiang, 2004).

All in all, whether director Zhang's intent was to arouse public attention toward rural education, or to get an "admission ticket" from the government, *Not One Less* had huge social impact and made people face the problems of rural education. It became a driving force to create awareness, promote changes in public thinking, and spark symbolic and concrete contributions to educational improvement.

THE SOCIAL RESPONSE TO NOT ONE LESS

After *Not One Less* was released and shown throughout the world, it received various awards from different Film Festivals and successfully drew people's attention within and outside China. Different people have different interpretations and reactions toward the film and have expressed thoughts and ideas through various channels. Some people even organized fundraising activities to help poor students in rural China.

After the release of the film, in 1999, both Wei Minzhi and Zhang Huike were recruited to attend a private middle school in Shijiazhuang. Their tuition fees were waived and they received 300 yuan subsistence allowance per month. The school also helped Wei Minzhi's parents find jobs (Fan, 2010). At the same time, the film also caught many people's attention in Hong Kong. Pan Jielian, who is among one of them, got in touch with Zhang Huike and adopted him as her son after she saw the film (Jiang, 2004). Later in 2004, professor Chen Ergang from Brigham Young University Hawaii came all the way to Wei Minzhi's university in Xi'an to talk to her and promise her that if her oral English could improve within a year then he would help her to study abroad, a promise he fulfilled in 2006 (He, 2007). The release of the film not only brought change to the leading characters' lives but also caused bigger influence on various areas in China.

In Mainland China, on the *Not One Less* Film Premiere in Qingdao on April 21, 1998, Ma Lunya, the deputy mayor of Qing Dao city, called on different institutions to organize leaders, employees, and students to watch this film. He mentioned that it is important to pay attention and give support to rural education in China (Sina, ND). Moreover, at the time of *Not One Less* release in 1999, the China Copyright Office issued a notice forbidding unauthorized production or distribution of the film, the first time China had enacted special copyright protections for a domestic film.

At the same time, it is reported that a stir also followed after the film was published in Taiwan and Hong Kong. Many people reached out and donated a large amount of money to kids in rural areas of China. Richard C.T. Lee, previous principal of Taiwan National Chi Nan University and Providence University, wrote several articles in 2002 stressing that *Not One Less* is a "famous film that caused a sensation throughout the world," and what was shown in the movie should be "remembered and remind us the similar situation in rural areas in Taiwan" (Li, 2002). The Hong Kong Institute for Integrated

Rural Development, which aims to promote social, cultural, and economic development in poverty-stricken regions of China through financial support, research, and project development, published an article about *Not One Less* on its website and asked for people's help in fundraising for other rural villages in similar situations (Shi, 2000).

The movie also received much praise from people all over the world. For instance, an internet user Lareail said, "I was a village kid just like them, and I think more concerns and attention from the public means more hope to people in rural areas.... no one should not be left behind by his/her country" (Lareail, 2013).

Please Vote for Me[3]

Released in 2007, Chinese director Chen Weijun's documentary *Please Vote for Me* attracted great attention. Part of Steps International's "Why Democracy?" film series, *Please Vote for Me*, found a place on the Academy of Motion Picture Arts and Sciences list of 15 "Oscar shortlist" documentary feature films. The film won the Sterling Feature Award at the AFI (formerly Silverdocs) Film Festival and was distributed to over 35 countries around the world. Yet this "nail-biting political drama about 7-year-olds" (Hesse, 2007) was banned by China's State Administration of Radio Film and Television (SARFT) and thereby prohibited from public distribution or viewing, though plenty of pirated DVDs can still be found in most video stores. Even director Chen claims to have bought several pirated copies of the film to send to his friends and family. "They did a good job pirating the PBS version directly," he laughed (Wei, 2012).

The 58-minute documentary depicts a "democratic election" of class monitor in a third-grade class of eight-year-old children in the Evergreen Primary School in Wuhan, China. It's a race among three candidates, Luo Lei, Cheng Cheng, and Xu Xiaofei, nominated by their head teacher. Under varying degrees of pressure and manipulation from their doting parents, the three candidates use all means to win the desired position.

Shorter than most documentaries, *Please Vote for Me* is still powerful. Director Chen spent over a year on the whole production process. To capture their authentic actions and to encourage their familiarity with each other, director Chen spent three months with the children before the official shooting took place (Cui, 2007). Over four weeks in 2006, director Chen recorded more than 100 hours of material. For over a year, scenes were edited to keep them brief but forceful.

What messages does the film carry and deliver? What are the reactions and responses from its audiences? Since the film is non-authorized within the People's Republic of China, does it have any influence on the society? These questions will guide the following discussion and interpretation of the film as a form of attempted leadership.

Please Vote for Me as discursive leadership

Like director Zhou's (*Senior Year*), director Chen reported documentary to be the most suitable and liberal way to express personal ideas and concerns and evoke public attention. It is clear that directors Zhou and Chen both sought to exercise public influence by highlighting social issues which, while important to themselves, may lack public awareness. Chen refers to the process and quality of documentary filmmaking as the "power of authenticity." It is the power to touch and resonate within the deepest part of an audience's heart. "Authenticity is the soul of a documentary," director Chen emphasized (Wei, 2012).

Actually, before setting his camera on issues related to kids and education, director Chen was well-known for making *To Live Is Better Than to Die*, the first documentary revealing an AIDS-tortured family's life in Wenlou, an "HIV village" in Henan, China. *To Live* was awarded a Peabody and Grierson award, as well as the Rudolf Vrba Jury Award from the One World Festival in 2003. Likewise, *Please Vote for Me* received over 15 awards, including a Grierson and an Emmy nomination. Five years later, in 2012, director Chen astonished the world with his new documentary *Education, Education*, which was screened by 70 national broadcasters worldwide, as a part of the "Why Poverty?" global documentary project (also run by Steps International). Director Chen's pattern of work indicates a desire to draw global attention to Chinese social issues through international organizations and platforms (Zhao, 2013). Asked about his direction, director Chen responded,

> I just want to make movies that can be understood by different people throughout the world. If people can resonate with my work, they would like to spread it out. And if it has been spread widely within the society, it will eventually get public attention with or without nominations in various film festivals.
>
> (Wuhan Weekly, 2013)

Chen thus believes the purpose of creating documentaries to be not merely "making a film and storing it in the filing cabinet," but to "encourage more people to watch and to reflect" on things they may not know or think about (Chen, ND).

Please Vote for Me strikes its chord, in Chen's words, by allowing audiences to "see the rules and regulations found in an adult society placed upon... eight to nine-year-old children" (Chen, ND). Interestingly, director Chen recalled that he initially hesitated and declined the invitation to produce the documentary, stating that it was "too hard to capture a story about democracy in China" and that "a documentary on politics in China would not catch many people's attention and sympathy" (Changjiang Business Daily, 2013; Chen, ND). Later, however, his casual talk with a colleague's son Cheng Cheng (who would later become one of the main characters in the film) triggered his new interest in creating *Please Vote for Me*. During that conversation, when asked about his dream and plan for the future, the eight-year-old boy replied without hesitation that he "wanted to be the President of the State" so that he would "be in charge of things," stating that if he cannot drive, "nobody is allowed to drive" (Yang, 2008). After having more talks with other children, director Chen discovered that most of them sought a government post. Teachers, it was believed, needed to "work hard on grades" and businessman might "risk a loss" (Wei, 2012). Director Chen found this odd as he recalled his own childhood when children seemed more inclined to seek careers as doctors, writers, scientists, and so on (Yang, 2008).

Chen pondered, "What make Chinese kids think and act in this way nowadays? Does that have anything to do with the social-political system?" Cheng Cheng coincidentally mentioned to Chen that he has an opportunity to "run for" the monitor position through a "democratic election" in the coming semester. This further prompted Chen to imagine what it would be like to place the political rules found in an adult world among children. With confusion and curiosity in mind, director Chen decided to address these questions with his camera so that audiences could draw their own observations and conclusions. His film might also initiate more questions and more reflection, which would "especially be useful for viewers with little interest in democratic politics – and they comprise the majority of the audience" (Chen, ND).

Messages sent by Please Vote for Me

According to director Chen, his initial intent in making the film was to see "the children's sense of democracy and collectivism" within a *suzhi jiaoyu* (quality-oriented education) pioneer school (Cui, 2007). At the beginning, by recording the process of the "democratic election," director Chen sought to show the audience the benefits and positive impact on children of this "creative and pioneer education activity." As production continued, however, various incidents occurred that altered the focus of the film and produced different layers of narrative and meta-narrative, thus stirring a variety of interpretations.

Political schemes and corruption

Although director Chen appealed to audiences not to "interpret so deeply" his film's "political meanings" (Cui, 2007), most of the responses and reactions to the film still focused on scenes depicting political schemes – and what could be considered corruption – carried out by the elementary school candidates. Despite director Chen's appeal, it is difficult to ignore the larger social parallels. The children (two boys and a girl) do not start out as "political animals" but seem gradually pulled into a system that seems to reward the use of fiscal influence.

For example, after the nomination by their teacher, Ms. Zhang, the two boys appear full of confidence and energized about the first-round competition of the election, the talent show. When the current class monitor, Luo Lei, is offered help and guidance by his parents, he refuses confidently saying that he will rely on his "own strength" and will refrain from "controlling others" because "people should vote for whomever they want" [00:05:23]. Lei later refuses his parents' help again. His competitor, Cheng Cheng, however, seems more open to receiving his parents' support. Bribed with a promise of extra TV time, he practices his most confident song for them, again and again. The only girl competitor, Xu Xiaofei, seems to be a little bit overwhelmed and afraid of the whole process, seemingly having no idea on what to do or say to classmates during the talent show. Gradually, under her mother's step-by-step lead and instruction, she builds up her confidence and a smile returns to her face. Little does she know, however, the "political machine" she will soon encounter.

Just before Xiaofei's performance in the talent show, Cheng Cheng is seen busily lobbying his assistant to "make some noise," that is, to boo after Xiaofei finishes her show. Even as she begins her performance, Cheng's followers jeer Xiaofei by first shouting out her weaknesses and then by simply shouting "overthrow Xiaofei." The high-pressure taunting causes Xiaofei to have an emotional breakdown before she can even begin her performance. After, perhaps, regaining his "conscience," Cheng Cheng comes to the head teacher and Xiaofei to apologize "on behalf of Luo Lei" (the other candidate). Prior to Luo Lei's performance the next day, we see the sadly familiar political scheme Cheng Cheng played – he asked Xiaofei to scream out Luo Lei's weaknesses and taunt him in revenge. As all the audience might wonder, how could an eight-year-old boy seem so tactful at playing political tricks? Cheng Cheng's words to Ms. Zhang reveal the answer, "My mother told me a trick last night, she said I should boo Luo Lei off the stage, and I am putting that into effort now" [00:16:56–00:17:05]. Cheng Cheng's mother's tactic seems effective. Soon after Luo Lei finished his performance, kids began shouting "Luo Lei, Luo Lei, always hit others; Luo Lei, Luo Lei, always threaten others; Luo Lei, Luo Lei, overthrow Luo Lei!" [00:17:49–00:18:01]. Cheng Cheng's tricks appear to work and his support seems to grow. Luo Lei grows frustrated and expresses his desire to quit the election. Simultaneously, Cheng Cheng grows more confident and continues lobbying his classmates by promising to give them some official appointments if he wins the election.

Cheng Cheng's mother is not the only "political operative" behind these candidates' back. In fact, compared to her, Luo Lei's parents' political skills are much more crafty and effective. Realizing Luo Lei's "underdog" status in the campaign, his parents can't sit aside and watch him worry. They sit him down for a long strategy session during which his father, a police director, and a supervisor of the city railway system offer to invite the whole class for a free ride on the local monorail. Luo Lei's father suggests this is a good opportunity for him to "show off" and "improve the relationship" with the classmates so that they will vote for him. Luo Lei agrees, and after the monorail outing, Luo Lei's "numbers" (based on his own survey) seem to shoot up. He happily tells his mother "those kids who were against me will now vote for me" [00:22:58]. Now it is Cheng Cheng who approaches the teacher with an extremely sad face saying that he wants to quit the competition, for he appears to have now lost a large amount of support.

By now it seems that the children's democratic election has evolved and escalated into a power competition and political battle among three families. The candidate's strongest financial and mental supporters during the competition, the parents tried their best to help their child win through all necessary means, which, of course, seem to reflect various real-life campaigns in which candidates strive to build any kind of voter *guanxi* (i.e., "you scratch my back and I'll scratch yours"). Thus, from time to time they need to make various enchanting and generous offers to secure uncertain votes. In order to gain and maintain the political power, bribery, corruption, political schemes, and empty promises can be seen in almost every electoral campaign.

The competition ends after three rounds of heated debates and a final speech among the candidates. Not surprisingly, both Cheng Cheng and Luo Lei's parents have drilled them what to say, how to argue, and how to react. Back stage at the debate, Luo Lei's father shows a "thumbs up" upon seeing his son follow his recommended moves. Moments later, however, Cheng Cheng follows his mother's strategies and successfully turns the situation around by calling Luo Lei the "dictator" who always "beats on" others. Now it seems that Cheng Cheng has won majority support by setting up an ideal model of the monitor to the class. Later that night, full of confidence, Cheng Cheng focuses on preparing his final speech in front of his parental "think tank." On the other side, Luo Lei's father takes out a pile of Mid-Autumn holiday greeting cards for every student in class – the "trump card" to buy off voters' hearts. Unexpectedly, although many students promise to vote for Cheng Cheng and show strong revulsion toward Luo Lei's "dictator" style of leadership, the result shows the majority votes (25 out of 39) go for Luo Lei.

No matter what initial plan director Chen had for his film, the appearance of *Please Vote for Me* provokes heated discussion and intense concentration on current political practice. On a special US Public Broadcasting System talkback presentation of *Please Vote for Me*, viewers with different backgrounds posted and expressed their thoughts and concerns on the internet forum. Some responses tied the film back to the American setting by affirming the similarity of the scenario in the film and the reality of current American political environment.

How interesting that the traits that make up today's American political candidates (and probably politicians all over the world) show up even in eight-year-old kids in China. The manipulative kids and parents demonstrate how early in life the ultra-competitive mindset is drilled into us.

(User named Dusti Chuang, Feb 8, 2008)

The competition, the selfishness, the needing to get ahead by any means. What better place than America to understand all of that was displayed in that classroom? What is it that we reward in this country that is so different than others?

(User named Benny Castillo, Jan 24, 2009)

Both posts raised critical questions and issues, speaking to the filmmaker's meta-message regarding the tremendous power of family background and social status on children's education and attitude. This influence emerges in other films, a note to which we will return in Chapter 5.

Different people observing the same events may derive different messages. For instance, some like red roses for their fragrance; some for their passionate color; some like it for their fresh taste; and some for their romantic symbolism. This is especially true when it comes to cinematic art; their stories conveyed with fascinating lights, images, sound, and music. More than mere gray words on white paper, films offer an expansive space for comprehension and interpretation. Through our personal thoughts and those of others, so many worthy fascinating issues arise: "democracy," "bribery," and more.

Democracy makes you turn against friends and people you love for something that you only want for the moment. Democracy isn't perfect, but it never had to build a wall to keep people from escaping it.

(Guest User, June 7, 2010)

Democracy means that everyone should be involved and never excluded from being heard. Everyone needs to be involved and interested in our government and, most importantly, feel confident that our opinion does count for something and will make a difference.

(User named Cynthia, Dec 20, 2007)

Once again money talks. It seems to me the winner's father had deep pockets, which equaled votes for his son. However, I thought both boys were pretty ruthless. But, then again, politics is hardball after all.

(User named Jeanette M. Johnson, Feb 1, 2009)

Sometimes, however, it is hard for people to hold back their personal presumptions and totally open their minds when trying to understand a different culture. People tend to interpret and add personal attitude to things with which they are not familiar. Perhaps that's why user Fish posted the following comment on talkback forum,

> I'm surprised that so many people's comments on here revolve around the whole concept of communism. The movie wasn't even about that, and it is presumptuous to think that the election was like this solely because China is a communist country.
>
> (User named Fish, Oct 23, 2011)

Those with more open minds and less proneness to initial judgments may see more than they expected and perhaps become more able to understand unfamiliar ideas and perspectives. Perhaps "Western democracy," in its extreme, does have a dark side, one that remains equally dark whether noted by Mao or Tocqueville! Should we not marvel that a film like *Please Vote for Me* provides a platform for a collage of intersecting, contrasting, and challenging ideas! The production of discursive leadership creates ongoing and unpredictable impact. Though the film's public presentation appears to be currently discouraged in China, its existence represents the increased interest and concern among Chinese filmmakers for social, cultural, political, and educational connections. The heated discussion about *Please Vote for Me* throughout the world attracted more audience and discourse, thus echoing director Chen's original ideas on the value of making influential film,

> I just want to make movies that can be understood by different people throughout the world. If people can resonate with my work, they would like to spread it out.
>
> (Wuhan Weekly, 2013)

As a documentary on the nexus between formal and informal student activity within an elementary school, audiences would be expected to pay great attention to education-related themes. In fact, issues related to education have often haunted director Chen, who has over the years shown great concern as well as grave doubts about China's current system. During an interview with *Southern People Weekly*, director Chen admitted a belief that most people don't know how to educate their kids. He included himself, confessing that he had been "kidnapped" by the current Chinese education system (Wei, 2012). In apparent response to his concerns, he uses his documentaries, first *Please Vote for Me* (2007), then *Education, Education* (2012), as "weapons" to problematize the issues he sees within the education system.

In *Please Vote for Me*, for example, Chen uses a series of extreme long and high-angle shots showing the practice of *guangbo ticao* (*broadcast gymnastics*) [00:25:47 & 00:46:33], a physical exercise program mandatory throughout all Chinese schools since 1952. Through the camera, audiences see all students lining up in straight rows doing the same moves according to the broadcast commands. The long, high shot selection renders the children as smaller, less significant and swallowed by the institutional setting (Fabe, 2004). By using these shooting techniques, director Chen suggests that within the Chinese education system, even an innovative school like Evergreen Elementary, with its democratic class election, differs little from other schools, subject to the same highly centralized drilling as all others.

Throughout the better part of *Please Vote for Me*, director Chen captures the election process by using medium shots from the eye level in order to re-humanize the children. It is interesting, however, to observe throughout the election process that their teacher, Ms. Zhang, is seldom involved in the children's activities, even when things seem to be sliding out of control. Viewers may wonder why Teacher Zhang allows the intimidation and bribery to continue. What of professional ethics? One ironic possibility is that Chinese education policies stressing "quality education" (*suzhi jiaoyu*) have prompted her to hand free control over to her students in this one arena of school social activity. One could also infer that in the pressure-filled exam-driven context of Chinese education, she has many other more immediate concerns. The children must learn to work their political problems out for themselves, just as do their older peers who must navigate through years of "testing hell."

Education, Education[4]

While director Chen sends out subtle social messages about Chinese education with *Please Vote for Me*, his later documentary *Education, Education* (2012) speaks them out in a more direct and critical way. Both films were supported by and included in projects run by the non-profit Steps International organization, which aims to "combine documentaries, new media, old media and outreach to get millions of people talking about big issues" (Why Poverty, ND). Chen had been planning on making both films for some time before he got the Steps project invitation. Thus, these two films represent director Chen's desire to problematize China's current education system.

Education, Education reveals the post-high school educational pursuits of three seemingly unconnected individuals. They are Wang Zhenxiang, a tutor from (the possibly shady) Hongbo Software Education College; Wan Chao, a new graduate from the newly established private Luojia College, Wuhan University; and Wang Pan, a rural village high school graduate who did not score high enough to enter public universities. The camera exposes a dreadful cycle of corruption and disappointment – especially for rural youth – apparently resulting from the rapid expansion of small private post-secondary educational organizations. Since the Chinese government allowed for privatized universities in 1997, the rapidly blossoming education industry is perceived by some to have gradually gone out of control and in many instances become infiltrated by con artists.

According to China's Ministry of Education, although a huge number of private colleges and universities have sprung up over the past two decades (allowing increased access for many high school graduates), the relatively loose academic credentials of many new colleges raised questions as to their overall legitimacy. Director Chen is somehow able to capture one such college's recruitment counselor disturbing confession.

> We (Hongbo Software Education College) are a private enterprise and not really a college. Strictly speaking, it is just a company. We attract the students, get their fees, and send them on their way. That's it. We don't teach them anything and the college doesn't care.
> [00:03:47–00:04:10]

Education, Education suggests that rural students, desperate to fulfil their "university dream," but with limited access to quality educational resources, may be more likely to be victimized by such shady operations. Wan Chao and Wang Pan, for example, scored low on their NCEE test and could not enter most public universities or colleges. Not only do they fall victim to sham institutions, but their families go into debt for several years to meet their extremely high tuition fees. Pan's parents go so far as to throw a "party" for their friends and families, who will be expected to donate money for her tuition.

Director Chen also turns his camera to expose what happens to those who manage to graduate from these sham colleges. Might simply having a certificate provide young people a better chance to find a job? Can a formal piece of paper open any doors? Director Chen tries to show us the answer through Wan Chao's experience. As a fresh graduate from "Luojia College, Wuhan University" (which viewers discover has no connection at all to the actual Wuhan University), Wan Chao has failed to find a job in Wuhan city despite having gone to several huge job fairs and delivered hundreds of resumes to all kinds of companies for positions that might or might not match up with his bachelor degree. Though he manages to pass some interviews and is offered a probationary training position, his salary can barely cover his monthly expenses. Life is cruel, however, and Chao is fired from two such positions during the documentary. Yet as the documentary ends, he is still trying his best to find a job while still living off his parent's support. *Education, Education* seems to plead with its audience: Not only has "education" (as a social institution) failed to provide a way out of poverty for millions of young Chinese, it also has led to the spawning of what amount to educational "traps" for them; places that suck away their resources and leave them with little flesh on the bone!

With *Education, Education*, director Chen expresses his concerns in a more direct way, using his camera as an explicit social tool. He stressed that the basic message of this film is to encourage all the "disadvantaged groups" within the society to honestly face what may amount to socialized and institutionalized oppression. Nevertheless, his words appear to soft-sell the problem:

> [The children] are our successors and the future of our countries. However, our societies and educational systems have complicated the growing-up process of children by compromising their simplicity and making their child-like innocence conform to worldly standards.
>
> (Chen, ND)

He also expressed hope that regardless of viewers cultural backgrounds, *Education, Education* will encourage audiences to think beyond the box and consider the flaws of a system in which they've always had faith. During an interview by *Southern Weekend Journal*, director Chen made his point clear, stating,

> A documentary cannot provide answers to every question. But if people who are poor or at the bottom of the society get a chance to see my film, they might start to realize that many individual problems are actually caused by the system and the "game rules." Then they might want to speak out and make some change – that is a way out of poverty.
>
> (Ji, 2013)

We thus conclude that director Chen uses film to create a new narrative and discourse; to transform an audience into a vehicle for social change. In an interview hosted by *Chinese Radio and TV of Amsterdam*, Chen expressed his expectations that,

> If *Education, Education* can touch officials' and rich people's hearts and make them pause and think about what they can do for the society, and help poor people rebuild their self-confidence by realizing their poverty may be caused by the system instead of themselves, it would be worthy.
>
> (Zheng, 2012)

From *Please Vote for Me* to *Education, Education*, director Chen has a worthy record of seeking to draw public attention to issues and problems that are systemic, largely hidden from view, or hidden "in plain sight." Though any actual systemic fix through individual or government efforts may be extremely difficult, realizing the existing problems is a first step toward improvement. One quote well-represents Chen's activities and attempts through these two films. He states, "sometime, you need to change the surrounding environment before you could make changes to your own life."

Country Teachers

Country Teachers presents us with a young woman's struggle and experiences as a substitute teacher in a rural village school in the early 1990s. The arrival of teacher Zhang Yingzi stirs up a series of conflicts and dilemmas for the peaceful little village and its only school, Jieling Primary.

Four regular staff work at Jieling: Principal Yu, Vice Principal Deng Youmei, guidance director Sun Sihai, and teacher Ming Aifen. The difficulties of obtaining sufficient funding from the county push Yu and his staff to falsify student enrollment rates. As an outsider unfamiliar with local culture and the terrible situation of the school, Yingzi's sense of justice prompts her to expose the truth to county officials. The result is a loss of funding for basic school repairs (as well as a loss of face for Principal Yu and his staff).

As Yingzi becomes more socialized to the local culture, economic climate, and the difficulties intrinsic to the school environment and local people, she begins to feel some guilt and some new respect for Principal Yu. She writes an article for the state newspaper, which draws considerable public attention and helps the school gain additional funding. We are presented with a happy ending as Yingzi and the other teachers finally begin to understand each other.

Country Teachers as discursive leadership

Similar to *Not One Less* and *Please Vote for Me*, the film *Country Teachers* as a narrative does not offer viewers any explicit consistent process of "educational leadership." Among the earliest Chinese films portraying the problems of rural schooling, with few exceptions, Country Teachers presents us with characters acting out of self-interest, reluctant to share information, thoughts, and ideas with one another. Despite its somewhat ethically neutral tone, Country Teachers has received praise throughout China for helping audiences "understand the extreme hard living condition of community-sponsored teachers" (Wu, 2007).

In a non-heroic fashion infrequently found in Chinese films of this period, *Country Teachers* presents a series of problematic issues common to many elementary schools in remote areas of China; scarce fiscal resources, high teacher turnover rates, high student dropout rates, and limited attention and concern from government officials and departments. The film and its director He throw these issues into the open air, suggest how they pose ethical dilemmas for these schools, and call for the attention of accountable public authorities. Why would director He decide to make a film about country teachers? What results did he wish to achieve? What is his main message or purpose behind the production of *Country Teachers*? We gain some insights from some comments he made in some later interviews.

Intention of the director

Shown in 1994, the film *Country Teachers* revealed the community-sponsored teachers' tough position in rural areas of China through the experience of the character Yingzi. Different from various other films on education topics in the early 1990s, *Country Teachers* is ripe with organizational and educational ethical dilemmas and defective teacher behavior, an extreme *avant-garde* product for its time. *Country Teachers* is not director He's first educational film. In 1992, with director Liu Baolin, he co-produced *Catch with Chaff*, a film that won huge positive audience feedback. Whereas the plot and flavor of *Catch with Chaff* seems humorous and ironic, the tone of *Country Teachers* is formal and grave.

In an interview ten years after the release of *Country Teachers*, when asked about the initial thoughts of making this film, director He described his self-felt obligation to bring "problems to the surface" so that more attention could be paid to the fact that "the hope of our nation relies on education." He stated that modern people tend to set their eyes on material needs and overlook spiritual ends, thereby resulting in a society run in an extremely rapid yet blundering pace. Believing that only education could solve this problem, He's camera serves as a tool for revealing his perspectives and opinions.

Rural school funding issues

The falsifying of student attendance rates at Jieling primary school could barely cover the cost of repairs, let alone teachers' salaries. This type of fiscal problem is often traced to (and aggravated by) the Nine-Year Compulsory Education Policy (NCEP) enacted in the late 1980s. According to the NCEP, all school-age children are required to have nine years of "compulsory, free, and unified" education regardless of whether they live in urban, suburban, or rural areas. The policy aims to alleviate citizens' financial burdens and cultivate nationwide social advancement. For rural areas, however, it was widely perceived that China's central government had failed to fiscally support the policy. Thus, the NCEP policy effectively imposed increased burden on rural schools, especially those relying on so-called community-sponsored teachers (those without formal training or certification).

The events in *Country Teachers* occur at the beginning stage of the NCEP and represent conditions and behaviors understood to be common at that time across poor rural areas; in particular, the use of tricks or subterfuge for gaining needed resources. Director He's insights, motivations, and creativity helped publicly expose this harsh situation, painting a narrative about the importance of primary education to a civilized society and how it had become an unaffordable "luxury" for many rural children. In the director's words, this was "the biggest threat to a nation's future destiny" (Ke, 2007).

Community-sponsored teachers' issues

Another acute problem depicted in *Country Teachers* involves the living and working conditions of China's rural community-sponsored teachers. These are a group of people who have played a very special and important role in the history of Chinese rural education. Due to the lack of national education finances, various community-sponsored schools were founded as "makeshift instruments for education expansion" in response to the educational policy of "walking on two legs" (Cheng, 1993; Robinson, 1991). From the late 1950s until the end of Cultural Revolution in late 1976, in accord with Mao Zedong's "Down to the Countryside (Shang Shan Xia Xiang)" movement, a vast number of knowledgeable young people were sent to remote rural areas in China and thus came to constitute the majority of community-sponsored teachers.

In 1992, under Deng Xiaoping's government, the ranks of community-sponsored teachers were reduced based on five principles; "stop, transfer, recruit, dismiss, retire." According to rough statistical research, however, the number of community-sponsored teachers reached 4,910,000 in 1977, thus making reduction in ranks quite difficult at best. Although most of the teachers wanted to transfer into the formal public system, the limited number of available openings produced intense competition. This competition serves as a key theme in *Country Teachers*, as the staff of Jieling school jockey for whatever slim chance exists for a regular public school teaching position. The news that the school would be granted one position ironically prompted distress among the staff over the decision as to which of them would be appointed.

Talking about these community-sponsored teachers and schools, director He expressed his feelings,

> I think the job they have been doing is so tough. Teachers are so dedicated to an education career, and especially these community-sponsored teachers. And some of them might encounter unfair things or bad things during their transferring process, but they own the children's appreciation and gratitude. Those kids who get out of the village would be grateful for having these teachers. And in many years when we look back, we would realize how great they were.
>
> (Ke, 2007)

Social influence

Released in 1994, *Country Teachers*, won several national film awards, including Best Film at two of the most important national film festivals, the 14th Golden Rooster and 17th Hundred Flowers Film Festivals. In addition, the actor Li Baotian, who played Principal Yu in *Country Teachers*, won three Best Actor Awards in a row at these same festivals, as well as from the SARFT for his break-through representation of soul and spirit for many community-sponsored country teachers.

Country Teachers' influence was not just reflected by these national awards but also in the attention it drew from the State Council Vice Premier at the time, Li Lanqing, who found it so "gripping and moving" that he used it to convey his concerns to other government leaders about the seriousness of the problem (China Business News, 2008). In Premier Li's memoir *Music, Art, Life*, he mentioned that

> The Cultural Revolution has passed for more than 20 years. It is time to deal with this historical problem and transfer those qualified community-sponsored teachers into the public education system as soon as possible. However, it is such an important issue that requires party and government leaders on all levels to pay full attention and carry it out.
>
> (China Business News, 2008)

To enhance its public impact, Premier Li contracted with CCTV to broadcast *Country Teachers* throughout the nation. Seeing the impact the film brought to the public, Premier Li showed this film to relevant government education officials to promote their comprehensive understanding of the problems. Leaders of the Party Central Committee and the State Council also viewed the film during a community-sponsored teachers' issues discussion conference. "All of them were so deeply moved by the film, and Premier Li Peng even shed tears."

Under this circumstance, the State Council leaders decided to grant community-sponsored teachers' salary and transfer issues a high priority, passing legislation in October 1997. As a result, by the end of 2000, 250,000 community-sponsored teachers successfully were transferred into the public education system.

Thus, although director He may not have anticipated the huge changes his film would foster, the film's influence was highly significant. As Premier Li stressed in his memoir, *Country Teachers* is a "wonderful artwork that contributed unexpected influence on the State Council committee's decision-making process of solving community-sponsored teachers' problems. Its existence helped accelerate the qualified community-sponsored teachers transferring process."

Summary

It is a researcher's good fortune to see things that exist, in a land where it is said they do not. Facing the beliefs and assertions of numerous East Asian educators and administrators appearing to limit "teacher leadership" to formally assigned tasks, we could not help but observe numerous examples shown in

Chinese films where people transcended those limits, expanding their influence within and beyond the school, into community and society.

In addition to the puzzle raised by the existence of such phenomena, the question arose as to "how would people realize it?" How could stories of "everyday leadership" enter the discourse of Chinese education theory and policy? One answer, of course, was contained in the very question we asked. Stories can be told through literature, art, music, cinema, and, of course, through book chapters.

In this chapter, we presented to the readers the embodiment and influence of untethering leadership in Chinese society through film as the media. By (1) analysis of the educational leadership demonstrated in six selected films, and (2) analysis of the discursive leadership demonstrated by film directors as storytellers, we've attempted to answer the core questions raised and echoed in this book. To wit, how do filmmakers express and depict behaviors, actions, or characters involved in mobilizing collective volition within Chinese policy environment? What messages do they seek to communicate to the public through film as visual rhetoric? Did the films bring any change or influence on the attitudes of lives of its focused audience? We hope you can find your own answer to these questions afterward.

Notes

1 Dialog and conversation in this subsection are selected and translated from the film *Pretty Big Feet*.
2 Dialog in this subsection has been selected and translated from film *Senior Year*.
3 Dialog in this subsection has been selected and translated from film *Please Vote for Me*.
4 Dialog in this subsection has been selected and translated from film *Education, Education*.

References

Boggs, J. M. (1996). *The art of watching films*. Mayfield Publishing Company.
Changjiang Business Daily. (2013). 陈为军：做纪录片的人，心要纯正. Webpage, http://jishi.cntv.cn/20130301/100074.shtml, accessed February 18, 2014.
Chen, W. (ND). Filmmaker statement on Please Vote for Me [Webpage], http://www.changjiangtimes.com/2013/03/434717.html, accessed February 18, 2014.
Chen, X. (2006). 周浩：从记者到影像制作人[Zhou Hao: From a journalist to an image producer] [Webpage], http://www.southcn.com/weekend/top/200606010009.htm, accessed February 17, 2014.
Cheng, K. M. (1993). *Zhongguo dalu jiaoyu shikuang (The realities of Chinese education in Mainland China)*. Taiwan Commercial Press.
China Business News. (2008). 李岚清与电影《凤凰琴》[Li Lanqing and the movie *Country Teachers*] [Webpage], https://business.sohu.com/20080103/n254439673.shtml, accessed March 17, 2014.

Cui, Y. (2007). 《请为我投票》入围奥斯卡 新浪娱乐对话陈为军[Please Vote for Me got nominated for the Oscar, Sina Entertainment dialogue with Chen Weijun] [Webpage], http://ent.sina.com.cn/m/c/2007-11-21/21491802165.shtml, accessed February 17, 2014.

Fabe, M. (2004). *Closely watched films: An introduction to the art of narrative film technique*. University of California Press.

Fan, J. (2010). 魏敏芝：中美友人对我故事的理解不太相同. Webpage, http://zqb.cyol.com/content/2010-07/22/content_3337856.htm, accessed February 24, 2014.

He, Z. (2008). 崛起美国：”谋女郎”魏敏芝追求梦想的人生传奇[Rise up in the United States: The life legend of Wei Minzhi's pursuit of dreams as a "Seeking Girl"]. The South of China Today, 2008, (6).

Hesse, M. (2007). Chinese film wins silverdocs award [Webpage], http://www.washingtonpost.com/wp-dyn/content/article/2007/06/18/AR2007061801706.html, accessed February 16, 2014.

International Herald Leader. (2011). 杨亚洲：我们对不起生活中的大多数[Yang Yaya: We are sorry for most parts of our lives] [Webpage], http://news.xinhuanet.com/herald/2011-05/25/c_13893121.htm, accessed January 21, 2014.

Ji, X. (2013). 你必须得上大学, 但是......纪录片《出路》中的"贫穷"[You have to go to college, but... the "poverty" in the documentary "The Way Out"] [Webpage], http://www.infzm.com/content/88435, accessed February 20, 2014.

Jiang, Y. (2004). 张慧科和他的香港妈妈[Zhang Huike and his Hong Kong mother] [Webpage], https://news.sina.com.cn/o/2004-02-21/08471857979s.shtml, accessed February 24, 2018.

Ke, X. (2007). "走出山村的孩子会感激你们"——访电影《凤凰琴》["Children who leave the mountain village will be grateful to you." - Interview with the movie Country Teachers] [Webpage], https://tv.cctv.com/2019/12/01/ARTI156BlKbpnFB2Cq3l9DDc191201.shtml, accessed March 15, 2018.

Kraicer, S. (2001). Not One Less. *Persimmons*, *1*(3). Accessed February 22, 2014.

Lareail. (2013). 不被理解的真实[Unrendered truth] [Webpage], http://movie.douban.com/review/5947401/, accessed February 26, 2014.

Li, J. (2002). 李家同博士[Doctor Li Jiatong] [Webpage], http://www.tbg.org.tw/tbgweb/cgi-bin/view.cgi?forum=30&topic=77, accessed February 26, 2014.

Lin, H. (2013). 周浩：寻找中国社会的节点[Zhou Hao: Searching for nodes in Chinese society] [Webpage], http://www.ihuawen.com/article/11793, accessed February 16, 2014.

Liu, J. (2007). 纪录片《高三》：记录高考用成长造句 [Documentary "Senior Three": Recording the college entrance examination and using growth to make sentences] [Webpage], http://media.people.com.cn/GB/40628/5839244.html, accessed February 14, 2014.

Mao, Y. (2011). Educational discourse in film: The history of Chinese educational documentaries. *Front Education China*, *6*(4), 620–638. https://doi.org/10.1007/s11516-011-0148-9

Rea, S. (2000). "In a Chinese village, the teacher is 13". *The Philadelphia Inquirer*.

Robinson, J. (1991). Minban schools in Deng's Era. In I. Epstein (Ed.), *Chinese education: Problems, policies and prospects* (pp. 163–171). Routledge.

Rosenthal, E. (2002). "Under pressure, Chinese newspaper pulls exposé on a charity". *The New York Times*. Accessed February 14, 2014.

Shi, Y. (2000). 兼谈一个内地山区老师和山区教育[Talking about a teacher and education in mountainous areas in mainland China] [Webpage], http://politics.people.com.cn/n/2014/0823/c70731-25522981.html, accessed February 24, 2014.

Sina. (ND). 一个都不能少主页[Not One Less Homepage] [Webpage], http://eladies.sina.com.cn/yige/, accessed February 24, 2014.

Southern Metropolis Daily. (2006). 获香港国际电影节"最佳纪录片奖"《高三》: 刻骨铭心的成长[Received the "Best Documentary Award" at the Hong Kong international film festival for "High School Year Three": An unforgettable growth] [Webpage], http://ent.sina.com.cn/x/2006-05-30/11211102642.html, accessed February 15, 2014.

Wang, S. (2006). 《高三》记录一段刻骨铭心的成长[Senior Year, recorded a period of unforgettable growth] [Webpage], https://news.sohu.com/s2007/gaokao30zhft/index.shtml, accessed February 14, 2014.

Wang, D., & Tian, X. (2004). 导演杨亚洲专访: 没劲的人讲述《浪漫的事》[Interview with Director Yang Yaya: The story of 'Romantic Things' by a Lossy Person] [Webpage], http://yule.sohu.com/2004/02/09/60/article218996074.shtml, accessed January 20, 2014.

Wei, Y. (2012). 陈为军: 记录难以接受的真实[Chen Weijun: Record the unacceptable truth] [Webpage], http://news.ifeng.com/shendu/nfrwzk/detail_2012_06/18/15379519_0.shtml, accessed February 16, 2014.

Why Poverty.(ND). Find out about poverty, watch amazing films [Webpage], http://www.whypoverty.net/en/, accessed February 18, 2014.

Wu, H. (2007). 天津: 创新思路拍主旋律电影 十余载结缘华表奖[Tianjin: Innovative ideas for making theme films, more than ten years of ornamental column Award] [Webpage], http://news.enorth.com.cn/system/2007/11/21/002368120.shtml, accessed March 15, 2014.

Wuhan Weekly. (2013). 陈为军: 在生命里寻求"真实的眼睛"[Chen Weijun: Seeking "True Eyes" in Life] [Webpage], https://news.ifeng.com/c/7fcRpJd4MW6?ivk_sa=1024320u, accessed February 18, 2014.

Yang, F. (2008). 一场完全透明的选举[A completely transparent election] [Webpage], http://zqb.cyol.com/content/2008-04/23/content_2154996.htm, accessed February 18, 2014.

Zhang, Xiaoling. (2001). A film director's criticism of reform China: A close reading of Zhang Yimou's Not One Less. *China Information*, 15(2), 131–139.

Zhang, Y. (1999) 张艺谋致函戛纳电影节[Zhang Yimou address to the Cannes Film Festival] [Webpage], http://news.sina.com.cn/living/9904/042004.html, accessed February 23, 2014.

Zhao, D. (2013). 纪录片《出路》的"解决"与"未解决":为什么上大学? [The "Solution" and "Unsolved" of the documentary "The Way Out": Why go to college?] [Webpage], http://jishi.cntv.cn/20130305/100097.shtml, accessed February 17, 2014.

Zheng, Z. (2012). 陈为军, 在拍全世界的问题[Chen Weijun, filming problems around the world] [Web log post], http://blog.sina.com.cn/s/blog_633f740e0101942v.html, accessed February 20, 2014.

5 Impossible mission V

To make the familiar new, and the new familiar

This book began with a puzzle, "is it possible to find an intuitive, and universal way to comprehend and unite the essence of leadership despite the language and cultural boundaries between China and the West" – that is, to gather and present evidence to support the argument that the concept of *lingdao* can be applied mean to strategies and actions occurring outside the structure of formal authority.

To investigate and understand this puzzle, popular Chinese films were identified featuring individuals and groups engaged in the mobilization of collective volition, and that included discourse or meta-language enciphered with the filmmaker's (or makers') intention to engage in social influence. In other words, we examined film meanings both denotatively and connotatively. The strength of denotative meaning lies in its close approximation of reality, to "communicate a precise knowledge that written or spoken language seldom can" (Monaco, 2000, p. 161). Film also contains connotative meaning conceived and embedded by the producing team. As Irving Singer (2000) writes,

> The communication present in cinematic art originates with a filmmaker who perceives reality through technological devices that are suitable for conveying whatever ideas and feelings he or she wishes to express. In the act of expression, reality is creatively transformed.
>
> (p. 7)

Compared to traditional Chinese written literature, bound by a lack of words to categorize or formally legitimize informal acts of *lingdao*, film has the capacity to restore, depict, and help clarify the authentic nature of heretofore undefined intentions and actions in direct, accurate, and comprehensive fashion.

The thick film descriptions offered in our prior chapter suggest evidence of the director's social intention and audience response to their messages. The purpose here was to demonstrate (1) how Chinese individuals and groups engage in acts aimed at mobilizing collective volition and (2) how the voices of the people, also a part of director's discourse, are heard, recorded, and spread out through the film medium.

DOI: 10.4324/9781032723778-6

Emerging themes

So far, if we see this research as a Chinese hotpot feast, then the previous chapters of this book were basically preparing all the necessary raw ingredients, suitable cookers, and doable recipes for the banquet. Thus, the main purpose of this chapter is to set up the dining table with all the carefully sliced and plated prepared ingredients, just the right flavors of hotpot soup-stock, personalized dipping sauce, and handy tableware for gourmets to begin an exceptional dining experience. Now, let us put all the ingredients into the soup-stock and dip into different sauce containers and see what kinds of flavor they would bring us.

The "flavors" offered here, that is, the themes, are served in two ways. First, they help consolidate this book's argument regarding the need to socially renegotiate the meaning of *lingdao*. But in addition, they are intended to steer readers toward extended ideas relative to the need for the further development and application of *lingdao* with respect to Chinese education. To accomplish this task, we will occasionally take the liberty to introduce ideas taken from films and other media not analyzed in the previous chapters.

The overarching themes dealing with leadership in Chinese education concern such matters as teacher-student relationships, financial issues, influential family factors, power of media, and importance of education. Regardless of the storylines, these themes serve as contexts for the exercise of *lingdao* outside the structure of formal authority as well as outside the arena of education policy. Taken as a whole, these themes formed a relatively comprehensive and in-depth expression on how people attempted to communicate, persuade, and influence others on certain issues, topics, or problems that they concerned, in a way to prompt change occurred within the society.

Teacher-student relationships

As it is shown in most all the sampled films, relationships between teachers and students tend to be affectively close. This is especially evident in two of the films depicting explicit informal leadership actions; Teacher Zhang in *Pretty Big Feet* and Mr. Wang in *Senior Year*. In both films, the "hero" exerts consistent effort to influence and change the minds of students by repeatedly talking sense to them in different ways and on different occasions.

In many Chinese films, teachers are the "parent" figure to their students. Teachers Wang and Zhang come across as authentic guardians of their students' best educational interests. For instance, Mr. Wang rushes to the bus station to discourage his student from leaving town. Certainly, this is an example of what Anthony Bryk referred to as the "extended teacher role" (Bryk et al., 1993), a characteristic vital to the establishment of a greater school community. Yet what is also quite important here is that Teacher Wang's actions were part of an overall effort to lead parents and others within his school community and thereby expand his *lingdao* into the realm of informal.

Similar characteristics are found throughout the sampled films, as with Principal Yu in *Country Teachers* and Teacher Wei in *Not One Less*. After much time, struggle, and learning, they earned trust and respect – and the suspension of judgment – from students, parents, and local community officials.

In addition to acting as caring authority figures, teachers have begun to be portrayed in some recent Chinese film and television as more of a friend or mentor figure. In other words, they are shown as primarily open-minded young professionals with creative teaching philosophies borrowed from the West. They strive to build an emotional connection with the students, gradually persuade them to view them as friends they can count on or turn to when they are in trouble. Examples of such portrayals include Teacher Gu on the TV show *The Shining Teenagers* (2002) and Teacher Fan in the film *Mark of Youth* (2013) (see Table 5.1).

Table 5.1 List of Films Depicting Teacher-Student Relationships in Chinese Educational Settings

Film title	Depicted teacher-student relationships (yes/no)	Traditional parent figure	Friend or mentor figure	Displayed leadership style
King of the Children (孩子王)	Y	√	√	Attempted leadership (failed); Discursive leadership
Her Smile Through Candlelight (烛光里的微笑)	Y	√	—	Attempted leadership (partly succeed); Discursive leadership
The Blue Kite (蓝风筝)	N	—	—	Discursive leadership
Long Ji (龙脊)	Y	√	—	Discursive leadership
*****Country Teachers** (凤凰琴)	Y	√	—	Attempted leadership (partly succeed); Discursive leadership
The Grass House (草房子)	Y	√	—	Discursive leadership
*****Not One Less** (一个都不能少)	Y	√	√	Attempted leadership (partly succeed); Discursive leadership
A Student Village (学生村)	Y	—	—	Attempted leadership (failed); Discursive leadership
The Shining Teenagers (十八岁的天空)	Y	√	√	Successful leadership; Discursive leadership
Balzac and the Little Chinese Seamstress (巴尔扎克与小裁缝)	N	—	—	Discursive leadership

(*Continued*)

Table 5.1 (Continued)

Film title	Depicted teacher-student relationships (yes/no)	Traditional parent figure	Friend or mentor figure	Displayed leadership style
***Pretty Big Feet** (美丽的大脚)	Y	√	—	Attempted leadership (partly succeed); Discursive leadership
***Senior Year** (高三)	Y	√	—	Attempted leadership (partly succeed); Discursive leadership
Little Red Flowers (看上去很美)	Y	√	—	Discursive leadership
Substitute Teachers (代课老师)	Y	√	—	Attempted leadership (partly succeed); Discursive leadership
Substitute Teachers (十三棵泡桐)	Y	√	—	Discursive leadership
My Career as a Teacher (我的教师生涯)	Y	√	—	Discursive leadership
Angel's Heart (天那边)	Y	√	√	Attempted leadership (failed); Discursive leadership
Feng Zhiyuan (冯志远)	Y	√	√	Attempted leadership (partly succeed); Discursive leadership
Chinese Schools (中国学校)	Y	√	—	Attempted leadership (partly succeed); Discursive leadership
Apology (道歉)	Y	√	—	Successful leadership; Discursive leadership
The Call of Maiji Mountain (麦积山的呼唤)	Y	√	—	Discursive leadership
***Education, Education** (为什么贫穷)	N	—	—	Discursive leadership
Mark of Youth (全城高考)	Y	—	√	Teachers strive for friendly relationships with students
Children at a Village School (村小的孩子)	Y	√	—	Attempted leadership (partly succeed); Discursive leadership
After School (放学后)	N	—	—	Discursive leadership
Looking Up (银河补习班)	N	—	—	Discursive leadership

*Films selected for in-depth written analysis
Bold type indicates original viewed sample

According to Table 5.1, we can see that 21 out of 26 selected films portrayed teacher-student relationship, and 90.5 percent of them depicted "parental" teacher-student relationship, among which, 5 films displayed a dual teacher-student relationship of parent and friend/mentor like. Only one of these films depicted a pure friend/mentor-like teacher-student relationship. All the selected films demonstrated leader-like behaviors among the main characters.

Though time and resources prevented such more recent works to be fully analyzed here, it is hoped that their existence will prompt further study of the teacher-as-informal-leader phenomenon.

Fiscal leadership

Among all the films in our data base, five of them set the camera toward the issue of resource scarcity. As shown in *Pretty Big Feet*, *Not One Less*, and *Country Teachers*, budget shortfalls cause various acute problems, including teacher shortages and low retention rates. In *Pretty Big Feet*, Ms. Zhang feels compelled to make an extreme sacrifice to obtain a computer for the school. The situation in *Not One Less* is even worse as the use of chalk is restricted to one stick per day. Our *Country Teachers* must work in an unsafe rickety school building and feel compelled to falsify student attendance rate to acquire funding to cover schoolhouse repairs.

Most families depicted by these films were in strained circumstances as well, and many students faced the decision of whether to drop out and support the family or stay in school to get education. Some, like Zhang Huike in *Not One Less* and the dropouts in *Country Teachers*, opt to quit school and go to work. However, several films depict student determination to become educated, attend university, break the cycle of poverty, and help their family move upward on the social ladder. This determination is shown to be at least partially rooted in the words of Teacher Zhang Meili; "Now you see the distance between our life and the city people's life. You have to study hard. There is no other way out, right?"

As it is shown in Table 5.2 below, 18 out of 26 selected films touched on fiscal issue. Most of the cases (19 films) were set in the rural areas of China. With a rather scarce educational, family and/or social resource, characters must struggle and fight against poverty.

Interestingly, in most less affluent areas of China, though a lack of money is a fundamental cause of education problems, it is also a driving force for local educational motivation and mobilization. However, a question raised among different directors through their films remains to be answered, that is, is education the way out of poverty? We discuss this question further under the theme "importance of education."

Table 5.2 List of Films Focused on Local Fiscal Status

Film title	Film focus region (rural/urban)	Depicted fiscal status (none/poor/middle/rich)	Fiscal leadership (none/attempted/effective/successful)
King of the Children (孩子王)	R	P	A
Her Smile Through Candlelight (烛光里的微笑)	U	—	—
The Blue Kite (蓝风筝)	R	P	—
Long Ji (龙脊)	R	P	E
*****Country Teachers** (凤凰琴)	R	P	E
The Grass House (草房子)	R	P	—
***Not One Less** (一个都不能少)	R	P	E
A Student Village (学生村)	R	P	A
The Shining Teenagers (十八岁的天空)	U	—	—
Balzac and the Little Chinese Seamstress (巴尔扎克与小裁缝)	R	P	—
***Pretty Big Feet** (美丽的大脚)	R	P	E
***Senior Year** (高三)	R	M	A
Little Red Flowers (看上去很美)	U	—	—
Substitute Teachers (代课老师)	R	P	A
Thirteen Princess Trees (十三棵泡桐)	U	—	—
My Career as a Teacher (我的教师生涯)	R	P	A
Angel's Heart (天那边)	R	P	A
Feng Zhiyuan (冯志远)	R	P	A
Chinese Schools (中国学校)	R	P	A
Apology (道歉)	R&U	P&R	A
The Call of Maiji Mountain (麦积山的呼唤)	R	P	E
***Education, Education** (为什么贫穷)	R&U	P/M/R	A
Mark of Youth (全城高考)	U	P/M/R	A
Children at a Village School (村小的孩子)	R	P	E
After School (放学后)	U	P/M/R	A
Looking Up (银河补习班)	U	M	—

*Films selected for in-depth written analysis
Bold type indicates original viewed sample

Family influential factors

Other than formal education institutions, the family typically serves as a child's first school, as parents begin to pass them knowledge. So what are parents' opinions on education? What are their expectations for their children? How do they influence their children? Within these films, directors tried to capture possible answers to these questions.

In *Please Vote for Me*, although the lens seems aimed at presenting a teacher's creative strategy for democratic understanding, it actually veers somewhat off-center stage to candidly reveal the tremendous interests and influences of parents, as well as the way in which individuals may be drawn toward corruptive strategies to obtain their goals. The parents of the three candidates not only provide strong financial and mental support but also seek to help their child win through somewhat questionable political means; attacking other competitors behind their back, bribery, and other "dirty tricks."

In addition to direct guidance or specific advice, the films show how parents can impact their child through unintentional behavior or habits. In *Pretty Big Feet*, for instance, Wang Dahe habitually plugs his ears with cotton to block his mother's endless high-pitched scolding and nagging. Parents' high expectation is thus portrayed as a double-edged sword to their child. On one hand, the high expectation might push the child to work harder. Sometimes, however, it might overwhelm the child and become a heavy burden. In *Senior Year*, out of stress and guilt that he might let his mother down ("she did everything to make sure I can get good education"), student Zhang Xingwang suffers an emotional breakdown and runs away from school two weeks before the entrance exam.

A Chinese parent and family can be the most loyal dream supporter for their child when it comes to a choice of university. In *Education, Education*, although the whole family is in poverty, Wang Pan's mother still borrows a large sum of money to send her daughter to a private university with expensive tuition fees. The same situation could be found in *Senior Year*, when a student's mother states that "as long as she wants to study and can benefit from it," they would even sell their house for their daughter to study abroad [00:19:00].

We've also listed the family influential factors as depicted within all the selected films in Table 5.3. As it is shown in these films, the parent-child relationship in China can be extremely close, as depicted in *Please Vote for Me*, yet can also become quite distant due to various reasons.

Different from the United States, one of the main reason that might prompt separation in Chinese parent-child relationships is the physical distance that can arise between them. According to the *2023 Rural Education Development Report*, there are still at least 9 million left-at-home children in China, although the number has dropped the 22 million reported in 2012. This group of children is known as *liushou ertong* (left-at-home children),

Table 5.3 List of Films Depicted Family Influential Factors

Film title	Depicted parent-child relationship (close/distant/ intertwine/none)	Pressure from family (high/ medium/low/ intertwine/ none)	Influence of family on education leadership (positive/negative/ intertwine/none)
King of the Children (孩子王)	I	L	P
Her Smile Through Candlelight (烛光里的微笑)	D	H	N
The Blue Kite (蓝风筝)	I	—	—
Long Ji (龙脊)	D	H	I
Country Teachers (凤凰琴)	I	M	I
The Grass House (草房子)	I	H	—
Not One Less (一个都不能少)	—	H	N
A Student Village (学生村)	D	I	I
The Shining Teenagers (十八岁的天空)	D	H	N
Balzac and the Little Chinese Seamstress (巴尔扎克与小裁缝)	—	—	—
Pretty Big Feet (美丽的大脚)	I	H	I
Senior Year (高三)	I	H	P
Little Red Flowers (看上去很美)	I	—	N
Substitute Teachers (代课老师)	D	L	P
Thirteen Princess Trees (十三棵泡桐)	D	—	N
My Career as a Teacher (我的教师生涯)	—	—	—
Angel's Heart (天那边)	—	—	—
Feng Zhiyuan (冯志远)	D	H	N
Chinese Schools (中国学校)	D	H	N
Apology (道歉)	I	H	N
The Call of Maiji Mounain)t (麦积山的呼唤)	—	—	—
Education, Education (为什么贫穷)	I	H	I
Mark of Youth (全城高考)	I	I	I
Children at a Village School (村小的孩子)	D	I	N
After School (放学后)	I	H	N
Looking Up (银河补习班)	I	L	P

*Films selected for in-depth written analysis
Bold type indicates original viewed sample

whose parents must make a living by working hard outside their hometown while the children remain at home. Sixteen out of 26 selected films touched the topic of left-at-home children, some of them focused on these children as main characters.

Jiang Mengjie, director of *Children at a Village School*, committed his cameras to call for more attention to the left-at-home children in rural China. In addition to *Children at a Village School*, he devoted two other films *Lu* (Road), and *Jia Yi* (a child's name) to focus on left-at-home children to help them gain more public attention. He stated,

> As more people saw the documentary The Road online and offline, and thanks to the reports of some kindly media, for the children, there were some material improvements indeed. But nothing can make up to the absence of their parents. There were still so many tough moments to face, so many hard questions to conquer, even harder. When asking the children about their dreams, one would probably get the same old answer, working.
>
> (Jiang, 2014)

The family's effect on a child is constant. It can deeply influence the way a child would look at the society, deal with problems, and perceive beyond parochial understanding. It is also an important factor influencing Chinese education, a form of social capital on which schools and teachers can rely, a form of fuel for further acts of teacher *lingdao*.

Importance of education

> The children are our successors and the future of our countries. However, our societies and our educational systems have complicated the growing-up process of children by compromising their simplicity and making their child-like innocence conform to worldly standards.
>
> Chen Weijun (ND), director of Please Vote for Me

For thousands of years, as Chinese people noted the value brought about by education, with teachers being highly respected figures in Chinese society. As it is described in several traditional cultural beliefs and old sayings, "书中自有颜如玉, 书中自有黄金屋" (Shū zhōng zì yǒu yán rú yù, shū zhōng zì yǒu huáng jīn wū – "the book owns the beautiful women, the book owns the house of gold"), which suggests that if you study hard you will become successful, a beautiful woman will want to marry you, and you will be able to afford to buy a big house. The spirit of this idea has been emphasized and passed down from generation to generation, especially for people of lower social status. For instance, in film *Pretty Big Feet* and *Senior Year*, both Ms. Zhang and Mr. Wang give encouraging speeches to stimulate students to "fight the way out" of the small village.

As a result, most of their students come to accept the belief that studying hard and going to college can bring a brighter future. The speeches in the film also serve as a continuous message to the audience about the acute importance of education in rural areas and, to some extent, their responsibility to help improve it. Moreover, the directors of *Not One Less* and *Country Teachers* state this purpose explicitly – to focus public attention on rural education and to steer related institutions to provide greater assistance.

Yet, more recently, one senses that people's faith in education has diminished for various reasons. A question might be haunting a lot of people – can education still bring the "gold house?" Impressions of disenchantment have been raised by various recent cinematic works. Their source of disenchantment may stem in part from ongoing efforts (since 1999) of Chinese education officials to greatly increase university enrollment rates as a means to alleviate employment pressure and stimulate domestic consumption and social contentment. Though such means and ends would seem to work in the interests of Chinese youth, some social critics have focused on the policy's downside.

For example, the film *Education, Education* presents viewers with a seemingly cruel reality: the proliferation of private universities offering a "shoddy product." These operations promise grand results, charge high tuition fees, but fail to provide any serious educational experience for students. In some ways, such operations serve as traps for rural youth seeking a well-paying job in the big city. An unauthorized Chinese film, *Blind Mountain*, recorded and revealed how a young "graduate" of one such operation struggled to find work to pay for her brother's education. Failing, she falls prey to a criminal gang and is sold as a bride in a remote area of China.

In a (2013) episode of *Morning Call* (a popular Chinese talk-show), writer, filmmaker, and show host Gao Xiaosong (2013) criticized the current Chinese education system stating that

> even if you study hard, you might not be accepted by good university. Once you got accepted by university, you might not be able to graduate. Once you are graduated, you might not be able to find a job. Once you find a job, you might not be able to keep it.

Though his comment seems sarcastic and informal, they mirror and echo the experiences of the young people shown in *Education, Education*. Wang Pan studied hard but cannot enter public university; those students who entered Hongbo Technology College could never graduate, because the school suddenly shut down; Wan Chao did graduate and was hired; but his lack of serious training prevented him from keeping any job.

Although these six movies focused on extremely different issues among different groups of people, there are still plenty similar signals, symbols, and elements emerging among the films analyzed in previous paragraphs. These themes might seem isolated from one another, but are in fact related, and as a whole serve as social critic to a fundamental question: can education really changes people's lives as it has always been suggested throughout Chinese history? If it is so, how can we make the education system perform this function more efficiently?

Summary

Difficult as it is to answer this question, it is significant that filmmakers continue to raise it. For example, in the 2002 film *Balzac and the Little Chinese Seamstress*, director Dai Sijie depicts the process of how during China's Cultural Revolution, an illiterate young country girl (known as "the little seamstress") became an independent lady with her own thoughts and opinions after being introduced to Western literature by two young relocated college students. In time, as the Cultural Revolution was ending (circa 1971–1974), she decides to leave her village to seek out "a new life." The film may be interpreted as suggesting how knowledge and thoughts have the magic to set people's minds free, change their concept of life, and gradually change their entire life experience. In the final scenes, however, her mentors express some sadness at the loss of the little seamstress and the sweet youthful innocence she represented.

Yet, as time passes, knowledge is much more accessible for most people in China. Moreover, the mechanisms of knowledge production are also more accessible. Though Chinese citizens may forever view the nation's higher status universities as the prime goal for striving students, can one not imagine a future in which education, productive employment, and respected social status can be obtained through more realistic means? Must the status and value of all private institutions of higher learning in China be perceived as, at best, questionable?

In this regard, the present study poses a peculiar irony. That is, while increased access to knowledge acquisition and production has rendered tremendous independent power and influence to writers, filmmakers, musicians, and artists, these do not tend to be considered "high status" careers for young people beginning their way in the world, at least, perhaps, by most parents. It is true that Teacher Zhang warns her students that college is the only way to avoid "growing potatoes in the same village over decades." Yet for the writer, filmmaker, musician, or artist who chooses to engage in social leadership, "college" may just be code for "education," introspection, reflection, and personal development. Indeed, it was previously noted in this study that the message of films like *Pretty Big Feet* is not aimed at rural citizens, but rather at a more affluent and socially secure audience. Is it too far a stretch to imagine the producers of such social narratives hope for, at least some day, for a far more critical public analysis of popular connected conceptualizations of "education," "occupation," and "social status?"

Each director discussed in this study apparently wished to make some contribution to Chinese people's social understanding. In each film, education serves as the focal point for public attention; as the arena in which people's attention may be focused on topics and problems familiar, yet strangely unfamiliar. The filmmaker leads by making people aware of a totally different side of a story they may have heard many times before. To paraphrase Samuel Johnson's adage, the filmmaker helps make the familiar new, and the new familiar (Johnson, 1908).

References

Bryk, A. S., Lee, V. E., & Holland, P. B. (1993). *Catholic schools and the common good*. Harvard University Press.

Chen, W. (ND). Filmmaker statement on Please Vote for Me. [Webpage], https://blog.sina.com.cn/s/blog_5898a7dc0100cc7m.html, accessed February 18, 2014.

Gao, X. (2013). The Unique Culture of the Han Nationality Part 3: The merits and demerits of the thousand-year imperial examination. 晓说[*Morning call*] [Talk show]. https://www.youtube.com/watch?v=XLCEF1vtk4c.

Jiang, N. (2014). 《村小的孩子》导演阐述[Director's explanation of 'Village Children'] [Webpage], https://movie.douban.com/review/6579080/, accessed June 24, 2023.

Johnson, S. (1908). *Johnson on Shakespeare*. Oxford University Press.

Monaco, J. (2000). *How to read a film: The world of movies, media, and multimedia: Language, history, theory*. Oxford University Press.

Singer, I. (2000). *Reality transformed: Film and meaning and technique*. MIT Press.

6 Ongoing mission
Generation-Z, always online!

In the 21st century, we have experienced a global financial crisis and the explosion of digital economy and technology finance, the iteration from social media to the "Metaverse," and an unprecedented global epidemic of Covid-19. At the same time, we've ushered in an unprecedented AI revolution. All of this has not only changed our views on international politics, social ethics, and fairness and justice but also changed our perception of daily life, social processes, and our imagination of the future. These changes are likely just the beginning of a lasting and profound transformation.

This transformation also lends itself to a further untethering of leadership, and supports our argument that the concept of *lingdao* mean much means much more than the strategies and actions of those in formal positions of authority. Throughout this book we've tried to demonstrate that popular Chinese film serves as a basis for this challenge, as we highlighted its assorted depictions of individuals and groups engaged in acts intended to mobilize collective volition. Moreover, we argue that the creation and distribution of a cinematic text represent a form of discursive leadership (Allan et al., 2006; Barge & Fairhurst, 2008), reflecting a filmmaker's effort to engage in social influence.

Most of the films examined in this study focus on Chinese school settings and thus relate directly to educational leadership. But we have also argued that the overall process of film creation and viewing can represent a form of educational leadership even for textual settings not directly related to schooling. In other words, acts of social influence can be viewed as acts of educational leadership.

Power of media

The power of media, internet, and computer on people's life has been highlighted in several films. In *Pretty Big Feet*, the internet and computer were introduced as trendy useful teaching equipment to help kids access knowledge they need. While in *Senior Year*, the online world so deeply attracted teenagers that two students would even climb the dormitory wall late in the night to surf the web and make money in online games. In *Not One Less*, the power of media helps Teacher Wei find the lost student and bring him back to Jieling elementary school. These are all examples of how socio-technological advancements often serve as double-edged swords. The eased instant access to internet and the capacity to send out social messages to vast numbers of people at one time is another example. Film itself, and the ability of filmmakers to complete their work and have it quickly distributed, can certainly be considered a sword whose direction and impact may remain uncertain for years or decades. Writing over 40 years ago, Jarvie (1970) suggested the nature of this vast power.

> Producers produce, audiences assemble, critics evaluate, and all because of the confrontation of people and the screen. Films are a peculiar communication channel: only a few outlet points, only intermittently "on," a cinema is more like a library than a water tap. The message is usually transmitted in a little over two hours. Darkness descends, the screen is lit, the film rolls and a world opens up.
>
> (p. 131)

If worlds could "open up" in the years prior to 1970, when cinematic communication was mostly intermittent, one must ponder what sorts of world opens up when nearly every individual holds the capability to create and distribute social messages instantly around the world. Certainly, as nations around the world work to develop new technological innovations, they must also ponder the leadership capacity of skilled sword-wielding masters of modern communication.

Always online, vibes on vibes!

While as we stepped into the digital era, We Media becomes the well-spread and mainstream platform for people, especially for the Generation-Z, to search for information, speak out, and exchange ideas. Ideas and information in new culture and art forms can be disseminated rapidly to the other side of the ocean through We Media platform such as TikTok, YouTube, Instagram, and others. Similar to the creation and distribution of a cinematic text, short videos contain messages and diffuse voices that can represent forms of discursive leadership as well. Through these short videos, Generation-Z can better understand different societies and culture, get to know the world, and broaden their horizons.

Unlike traditional media, including the art form of film, We Media provides with everyone both freedom and platform to express views and ideas through short videos. It plays an important role in information dissemination, while at the same time, people can expand their social influence by accumulating fans and influence on the platform. The convenience of self-production

110 *Ongoing mission*

and expression of authentic individual perspective through "mini-films" allows people a chance to attempt the mobilization of collective volition.

According to a Pew Research Center report, *Teens, Social Media and Technology 2022* (Vogels et al., 2022), 97 percent of surveyed teenagers say they use the internet every day, with nearly half of them saying they often stay online. YouTube remains the most used online platform for teenagers, with 95 percent of respondents stating that they access it via websites or mobile applications. In addition, the usage rates of TikTok, Instagram, and Snapchat are similar, at 67, 62, and 59 percent, respectively, and show a steady growth trend, as shown in Figure 6.1.

It is worth noting that in the past decade, the usage rate of some popular social media platforms has significantly declined. For example, comparing survey data from 2014 to 2015, Twitter usage rate decreased from 33 to 23 percent; Tumblr has decreased from 14 to 5 percent. Platforms known as Vine and Google+, however, have completely faded out of the sight of teenagers.

The decline in Facebook's teen usage is most noticeable. In previous surveys, 71 percent of teenagers reported using the software, but in this survey usage dropped to just 32 percent. According to the data reported by Pew

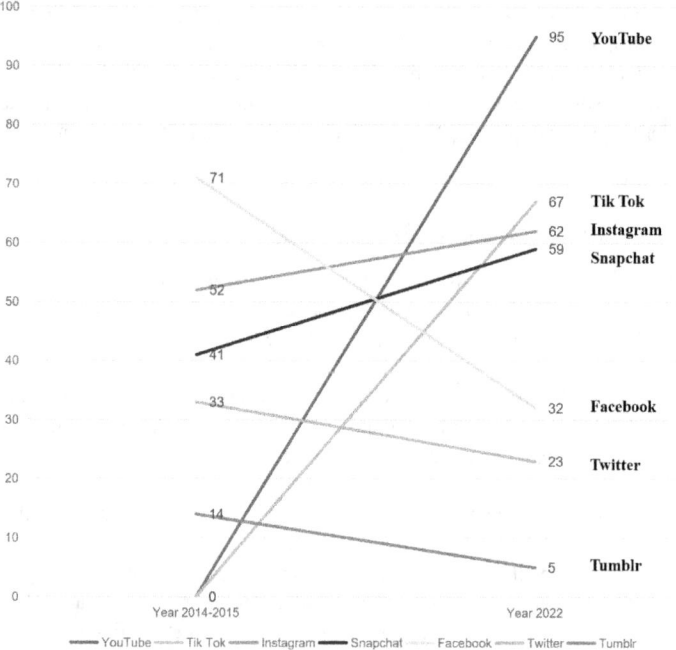

Figure 6.1 The Usage Rates of We Media among Teens in U.S.[1]

Research Center, Generation-Z is more dependent on social media than previous generations. Fifty-five percent of respondents believe that spending time on social media is a "wise choice." Thirty-five percent of respondents reported a high frequency of use.

When asked about "how to view the time spent on social media," 53 percent of respondents believe that they have spent too much time on social media; 28 percent said they allocate time to different types of platforms and applications. Among the youth respondents who "spend a long time online," 51 percent said reported spending too much time on social media; 26 percent reported social media as their only reason for going online.

The Pew study also reported that about 18 percent of the respondents found it very difficult to leave social media. Only 20 percent found this to be very easy. For teenagers, the more social media platforms they use, the harder it is to give them up. Among respondents who registered for more than one social media account, 32 percent admitted it was "difficult to leave social media."

Like the portrait of America's Generation-Z, *Yi Magazine* conducted a survey on *New Generation, New Proposition – 2022 Yi Magazine's "Big Survey" of the 2000s* of China in 2022.[2] Through a randomly selection of a total of 1041 post-00s, from over 30 provinces in China, and ranging in age from 14 to 22 years old (the so-called internet natives). This study focused on understanding the following five dimensions of the post-00s' lives: personal, learning, workplace, consumption, and culture.

Within the *Yi Magazine* sample, about 77 percent were familiar with the internet since childhood and have owned their own smartphones since elementary school. In the survey, WeChat (88 percent), Bilibili (66 percent), Weibo (57 percent), QQ (42 percent), and Xiaohongshu (40 percent) were the five most used social media platforms among post-00s. In addition, the official account and headline in WeChat app and Sina Miniblog (Chinese Twitter) have replaced the traditional media channels and become the main channels for post-00s to obtain non-entertainment information. Less than 1 percent post-00s chose newspapers as the main channel to obtain such information.

At the same time, the internet had a significant impact on shaping post-00s' knowledge system. When these internet natives were asked to name their cultural idols, Luo Xiang (who became popular through video lectures) ranked first at 11 percent. The online learning mode during the Covid-19 epidemic has to some extent strengthened their habit of online learning, especially through video, mini-films, and talk-shows. In this era of change, both schools and enterprises need to be prepared to adapt to the situation when planning education and training for the post-00s. Video-based teaching, enhancing interface interactivity, and adopting faster and fragmented communication forms seem to have a profound leadership impact upon the post-00s.

Another survey, Deloitte's 2019 report on *Media Consumption View of the Post-00s: Entertainment+Mobile+Social+Digital*, watching films (59 percent), listening to music (54 percent), and playing games (49 percent) are the three favorite entertainment activities for the post-00s.[3] In addition, for the post-00s, online socializing has largely replaced the need for face-to-face communication. The post-00s have an apparent strong desire to expand their "social chain" and acquire a solid sense of belonging.

According to a report on *The Post-80s, Post-90s and Post-00s Generation on TikTok*[4] (Ocean Engine Insights Center, 2019), the "target group index" (or TGI; a ratio comparing a target-group preference to that of the overall population), measuring rates of "likes" for short internet videos indicates a substantial increase across recent generations (i.e., from post-80s, to post-90s, to post-00s). In addition, the post-00s appear to have a wider range of interests and are more willing to subscribe and interact with the others through online platforms. This includes being more likely to download and recommend videos compared to the other generations. This might also suggest they are more likely to generally influence and lead.

To some extent, media usage habits shape the impact of media information on an audience (Althaus & Tewksbury, 2000). Since the audience needs to rely on media to obtain information for personal life, work, and social purposes, the greater an individual's dependence on media, the more important and influential media information becomes for them (Ball-Rokeach, 1998; Riffe et al., 2008).

As for the Generation-Z, or the post-00s, the information-gathering process changed due to the expansion of We Media platforms. Due to the huge amount and complexity of information offered by these platforms, selective contact has become more difficult to achieve. While gathering information, people may intentionally or unintentionally come into contact with various types inconsistent with their original beliefs. Information inconsistent with existing beliefs may have much less impact (Yu et al., 2012).

Thus, the development of the media itself, along with resulting changes in information dissemination channels and content, will also continuously regulate the influence of media information on the Generation-Z audience. A question arises as to how the interaction of public cognition, concepts, attitudes, and behavior might shape the efforts and effects of *lingdao*.

Leading while surfing

In the era of new media, a borderless, cross-regional, and popular open communication platform relying on new internet technologies has rapidly formed. Everyone can be a disseminator of information and influence. As Charlene Li discussed in her book named *Open Leadership: How Social Technology Can Transform the Way You Lead*, leaders can only ensure that they do the right things and do things correctly by actively and effectively using new media to improve their leadership style and enhance their leadership abilities with an open mindset.

In this era, the shortcomings of information acquisition, such as dryness, delay, and non-interactivity, can be easily overcome. By using digital and network technologies, We Media has reduced audience disadvantages in terms of the amount of information quantity and quality of information. New technology ensures timely – and targeted – communication, exchange, and feedback among multiple audience groups. Interaction models may thus become more effective as users tune in – or tune out – according to preference.

Persons and groups can create mini-films – essentially small bits of cinema – varying widely in terms of creativity, popular reach, and public influence. We can all be disseminators, expressing views across a range of social topics and current events, interacting with (perhaps often arguing with) others. On one hand, this kind of interaction and collision may promote positive change and be good for us all.

On the other hand, however, a problem arises. We've argued that leadership – and *lingdao* – involve not only the mobilization of volition but also the changing of minds. Does the pattern of We Media information diffusion described here actually produce a changing of minds? Or does it just solidify existing mindscapes in ways that may conflict with democratic social interaction? Do we become more open? Or more isolated?

Surfing the Pacific Ocean

A major rationale for this study relates to globalization and institutional isomorphism. The environment for understanding organizational and educational theory increasingly transcends national boundaries. Concepts and practices once held as constant become negotiable, problematized, and contested. New patterns of thinking flow like Wi-Fi waves back and forth across the Pacific Ocean. "School reform," as it emerges and evolves in both China and the United States can thus be thought of as a "wave packet" with the potential to upset the cultural, philosophical, and practical equilibrium set within traditional structures of leadership thought. As Shouse and Lin (2010) discovered, Taiwan's school principals who were hesitant to apply the concept of "teacher leader" beyond the classroom nevertheless used other words in expressing hope that their teachers would show leadership in helping to implement the complex demands of school reform.

With the arrival of the new media era, the media for information transmission has evolved from traditional paper prints, music, and film to emerging digital imaging media and future meta-images. What changes is the communication form and way of attempted leadership, while what remains unchanged is the leadership behavior of people attempting to change others' ideas and persuade them. Taken together, the implication appears to be that leadership – and *lingdao* – is, but is not necessarily always, a function of formal authority;

that from time to time, "leaders" can emerge from among the ranks of Chinese citizens; and that this represents a desirable social phenomenon within Chinese society. Therefore, a major goal of this book was to problematize and reconstruct the concept of *lingdao*. We started this task after noting the existence of a phenomenon – the informal exercise of social persuasion – that seemed to lack any Mandarin word to represent it. We continued the task with a focus on cinematic depictions of school and educationally based examples of informal social persuasion. We first framed this as an "impossible mission," the seeking of imaginary qualities, the challenge of "surfing across the Pacific." More directly, we sought to distil and change culturally situated meanings of leadership and, especially, *lingdao*. We no longer believe this to be impossible.

Notes

1 Vogels, E. A., Risa G., & Navid M. (2022). *Teens, social media and technology 2022*. Pew Research Center. Retrieved from https://www.pewresearch.org/internet/2022/08/10/teens-social-media-and-technology-2022/, accessed February 18, 2023.
2 Yi Magazine. (2022). *New generation, new proposition – 2022 First Financial's "Big Survey" of the 2000s*. Retrieved from https://m.yicai.com/news/101466288.html, accessed June 10, 2023.
3 Deloitte. (2019). *Media Consumption View of the post-00s: Entertainment+Mobile+Social+Digital*. Retrieved from https://socialbeta.com/t/104238, accessed June 10, 2023.
4 Ocean Engine Insights Center, 2019, The Post-80s, Post-90s and Post-00s Generation on Tiktok. Retrieved from https://trendinsight.oceanengine.com/arithmetic-report/detail/195, accessed June 13, 2023.

References

Allan, E. J., Gordon, S. P., & Iverson, S. V. (2006). Re/thinking practices of power: The discursive framing of leadership in the chronicle of higher education. *The Review of Higher Education*, *30*(1), 41–68.

Althaus, S. L., & Tewksbury, D. (2000). Patterns of internet and traditional news media use in a networked community. *Political Communication*, *17*(1), 21–45.

Ball-Rokeach, S. J. (1998). A theory of media power and a theory of media use: Different stories, questions, and ways of thinking. *Mass Communication and Society*, *1*(1–2), 5–40.

Barge, J. K., & Fairhurst, G. T. (2008). Living leadership: A systemic constructionist approach. *Leadership*, *4*(3), 227–251.

Deloitte. (2019). *Media Consumption View of the post-00s: Entertainment+Mobile+Social+Digital*. Retrieved from https://socialbeta.com/t/104238, accessed June 10, 2023.

Jarvie, I. C. (1970). *Movies and society*. Basic Books.

Ocean Engine Insights Center. (2019). *The Post-80s, Post-90s and Post-00s Generation on TikTok*. https://www.sohu.com/a/364870316_712171.

Riffe, D., Lacy, S., & Varouhakis, M. (2008). Media system dependency theory and using the internet for in-depth, specialized information. *Web Journal of Mass Communication Research, 11*(1), 1–14.

Shouse, R. C., & Lin, K. P. (2010). *Principal leadership in Taiwan schools*. Rowman & Littlefield Publishers.

Vogels, E. A., Gelles-Watnick, R., & Massarat, M. (2022). *Teens, social media and technology 2022*, Pew Research Center. Retrieved from https://www.pewresearch.org/internet/2022/08/10/teens-social-media-and-technology-2022/, accessed February 18, 2023.

Yi Magazine. (2022). *New generation, new proposition -2022 First Financial's "Big Survey" of the 2000s*. Retrieved from https://baijiahao.baidu.com/s?id=1737568886282275967&wfr=spider&for=pc, accessed June 10, 2023.

Yu, K., Stith, A. L., Liu, L., & Chen, H. (2012). *Tertiary education at a glance: China* (Vol. 24). Springer Science & Business Media.

Conclusion

How does one justify or explain a book that connects leadership theory and Chinese moviemaking? It's a long story, but one that can be summarized in the form of a short story. Here goes. There was once an American professor who became fascinated with leadership, particularly informal leadership, and its expression in everyday life. To him, this was not such an odd pursuit, primarily because the word "leadership" had such broad meaning and application in the United States, until he found his graduate students from the other side of the world all tending to hold a completely different understanding and cognition on the very same word!

We tried to tell a story to the audience starting from one day during a conversation the professor was having with one of his Chinese students. The professor spoke about informal leadership and what a good idea it would be if someone will research how it worked in Chinese schools. After several minutes of this, the Chinese student seemed puzzled and said, "I don't know what you mean."

Not long later, a similar question was asked of a sample of Taiwan school principals (using the Mandarin word for leadership, *lingdao* and/or *lingdaoli*) – "how do your teachers show leadership?" A similar response was given – "What do you mean?" After probing a bit, one principal replied that her teachers showed leadership by "moving up the ranks" from teacher to department head, to dean, to assistant principal, etc. The professor began to understand that, in Chinese culture, to be a "*lingdao*" or to show "*lingdaoli*" one needed to possess formal position. "*Lingdao/lingdaoli*" was fundamentally viewed as a downward flow of authority. "Does informal leadership exist in Chinese culture? Is there a relatively good Mandarin phrase existed to describe this type of informal social action?" With questions in mind, the professor gradually found answers through the addition of several movies to his educational leadership course syllabus.

At an early career point, this professor was moved by a paper presentation from Australian scholar Ross Thomas, "As they are Portrayed: Principals in Film," which analyzed examples of how these school "leaders" were presented in popular cinema. His examples included films such as *Clockwise* and *Picnic at Hanging Rock*, two films in which the principal role had little to do with school management, let alone with school "leadership."

Being a film buff, the young professor noted that schools, principals, and teachers often served the plots of filmmakers in ways more relevant to the practice of leadership, yet not directly tied to traditional formal schooling processes. In *To Sir with Love*, for instance, teacher Mark Thackeray's effort to prepare his students for adult life prompts him to virtually abandon the formal curriculum and to forge more personalistic (yet risky) relationships with his students. Thus, it came that *To Sir with Love* became a mainstay of the young professor's Introduction to Educational Leadership course.

This led, however, to an unavoidable idea – if "educational leadership" could emerge when teachers fractured the traditional walls and boundaries of formal schooling, could it not also emerge from settings entirely outside what we normally think of as "the school?" And were not such examples prevalent in literature and other media? Consider Jimmy Stewart's portrayal of Ransom Stoddard in John Ford's classic work, *The Man Who Shot Liberty Valance*, a greenhorn lawyer who risks his life to teach a group of disconnected townspeople about the value of lawful community.

"It started to make sense to me!" A graduate student from China expressed her excitement to the professor after the "film" class showing of *To Sir with Love*. "I think I finally understand the concept of leadership in the western culture through the film shown in class! And I believe Chinese movies portrayed such presentations of western leadership in ways that seemed to extend beyond formal roles and structures."

This led to one of those glorious emotional scholarly moments, the likes of which referred to by John Dewey – "...a troubled, perplexed, trying situation..." (cited in Kerlinger, 1986). For the professor knew that Chinese literature – and film in particular – were filled with narratives of ordinary citizens demonstrating what would in America and many other parts of the West be considered "leadership."

Together over time, the graduate student (that's me, your author) worked with the professor (my coauthor) to compile a list of movies, especially Chinese movies, in which schools, principals, and teachers were portrayed in ways more expressive of leadership, but in ways that seemed to extend beyond formal roles and structures. His favorite example, *To Sir with Love*, for instance, follows teacher Mark Thackeray's efforts to prepare his students for adult life by virtually abandoning the formal curriculum and, at times, by violating social and institutional norms. I, in turn, introduced him to *Pretty Big Feet* and *Country Teachers*, films in which Chinese teachers struggle, fail, yet are eventually redeemed or heralded not because they are effective in the classroom, but because they have changed hearts and minds beyond it. When viewed as case studies, we concluded, such narratives obscure the lines between formal and informal acts or status and thereby serve as expressions of discursive educational leadership.

In push this idea further, Chapters 1 and 2 addressed the different understandings and slippery nature of the "leadership" concept, in the social contexts of both the United States and China. On one hand, Chinese literature – and film in particular – are filled with narratives of ordinary citizens demonstrating what would in America and many other parts of the West be considered "leadership." But on the other, not only were such acts not considered *lingdao*, there was (at least as of around 2020) no other Mandarin word to describe this sort of leadership, which in this book we refer to as "untethered."

As of this writing, the idea of informal leadership has gained some of traction in China, especially in the arena of public schooling. For example, the title of "backbone teacher" (*gugan jiaoshi*) is now applied to teachers who show substantial skill in implementing the new classroom practices called for under Chinese educational reform. Interestingly, however, this again amounts to the granting of formal title rather than the recognition that the exercise of *lingdao* might be a natural human tendency.

We thus are led to three questions that served to drive our study. First, if Chinese people in all ranks of life are naturally disposed to engage in untethered leadership, then why has Chinese culture and language resisted its recognition? Of course, the same may be said for other cultures and languages which, for example (and unlike Mandarin Chinese), have one single word representing both "leadership" and "management." This phenomenon is referred to by linguists as a semantic gap.

Second, if movies (in a general case and in a specific case Chinese movies) move viewers to consider and possibly embrace ideas and actions previously considered wrong, impossible, or unnecessary, can one not suggest that an act of leadership – educational leadership – has occurred?

Finally and more globally, if films and filmmakers serve this function, does this not lead to an expansion of the concept of the "educational leader?" Can one not argue that educational leadership is not an activity confined to school teachers, principals, superintendents, or other educational officials? Put another way, can we accept the fact that educational leadership exists in wide-ranging film narratives created to move groups and individuals toward new ways of thought and social development? Put yet one further way, can we accept the concept that filmmakers may sometimes serve as educational leaders? In order to discover answers to these questions, we offered Chapters 3–5 to cover this idea.

We've heard it claimed (typically by professors in the field) that arguments like ours open the door to the notion that leadership, or educational leadership, means "everything." This is certainly not the case. But we do insist that the concept does not exist only behind gates, inside brick buildings, or within legislative bodies. With Chinese cinema serving as its focus, this book aimed to raise awareness of the presence of untethered leadership in education and in our world as a whole. It is a researcher's good fortune to see things that exist, in a land where it is said they do not. Facing the beliefs and assertions of numerous East Asian educators and administrators that appeared to limit "teacher leadership" to formally assigned tasks, we could not help but observe numerous examples where Chinese teachers transcended those limits, expanding their influence within and beyond the school, into community and society.

In addition to the problem of the existence of such phenomena, the question arose as to "how would people realize it?" How could stories of "everyday leadership" enter the discourse of Chinese education theory and policy? One answer, of course, was contained in the very question we asked.

Stories can be told through literature, art, music, cinema, and, of course, through doctoral dissertations. The storytellers, in this study the filmmakers, amplify the acts and experiences of individuals to larger audiences. The film serves as a form of social meta-analysis by gathering and condensing unseen data in ways that enlarge public experience and the potential for critical public thought. In this way, the story transposes "everyday leadership" into discursive leadership. Stepping into the Information Age, different forms of media emerge due to the development of We Media platform. Mini-films, short videos devoted by creators, people who were once just part of an audience become players on a new and changing field. How do We Media influence the Generation-Z's daily life? Do they recognize and try to show leadership through these new media forms? We discussed this with readers in Chapter 6.

So is the case with the whole book. By examining and problematizing Chinese conceptions of *lingdao*, we hope to enlarge the discourse surrounding them, particularly as they relate to Chinese schools and educational reform. At the same time, this is not the type of study from which policy recommendations can readily flow. Indeed, the very idea of a policy recommendation within the centralized structure of Chinese education seems to contradict the idea of informal localized *lingdao*.

The research implications of the book also seem a bit complex. Though we plan to continue exploring the ideas presented here, it seems clear that further empirical research into concepts such as "teacher leadership" or "informal leadership" in East Asian settings will influence the social reality of such settings. In other words, surveying Chinese educators regarding perceptions of teacher leadership can surely help to affect their perceptions.

120 Conclusion

Thus, what is offered here is the defense of a specific and, we believe, liberating conceptualization of leadership. It is an idea that fits within a strand of understanding within the literature that holds "leadership" as a process relatively independent from "leaders." Besides defending these ideas, we hope to amplify them and in some small way help spread them within Chinese organizational thought and discourse; for as Laurie Anderson was cited earlier, "language is a virus." So, it appears, is *lingdao*.

Index

Note: Page numbers in bold denote tables.

Academy of Motion Picture Arts and Sciences 79
AI (artificial intelligence) 108
Anderson, Laurie 34, 120

backbone teacher see *gugan jiaoshi*
Balzac and the Little Chinese Seamstress 17, 27, **42**, **98**, **101**, **103**, 106
Barnard, Chester 21, 24, 28
Blind Mountain 105
Bryk, Anthony 97

Cannes Film Festival 73
Cardano, Gerolamo: *Ars Magna* 1
Chen, Weijun 79, 80–81, 83, 85–88, 104
China: CCTV (China Central Television) 64; cinema 3–4, 6, 7, 17, 26–27, 40–41, 64; community sponsored teachers 89–92; Copyright Office 78; Cultural Revolution 41, 91, 92, 106; education reform 6, 14–15, 113, 118, 119; "face" 11, 26; history 1, 4, 7, 11, 20, 25, 32, 105; literature 4, 7, 9, 20, 32, 96, 117, 118; NCEE (National College Entrance Exam) 64, 65–67, 70–72, 87; NCEP (Nine Year Comprehensive Education policy) 90; rural education in 5, 6, 67, 74, 75–79, 86–87, 89, 90–91, 100, 104–105; university enrollment 105; SARFT (State Administration of Radio Film and Television) 41, 79, 91–92; Taiwan 5, 14, 32, 78, 116

China Gate 67
China Prep 67
Chinese School 67
Cinema 2, 4, 5, 10, 17, 26, 27, 34, 37, 40; Chinese 3–4, 5–6, 17, 26–27, 41, 64; as discursive leadership 6, 7, 15, 17, 26–27, 41, 45, 55, 65–68, 72–73, 77, 85, 93, 98–99, 108, 109, 118–119; documentary 7, 27, 40, 41, 64–65, 68, 75, 79, 80, 88; techniques 36–37, 44, 46–51, 85–86; *see also* filmmaking
Clockwise 4, 117
collectivism 11, 25, 32, 81
Coleman Report 16
Country Teachers 6, 10, **42**, **43**, 89–92, 98, 100, **101**, 103, 105, 117: CCTV and 92; Li Lanqing and 92
creativity 12, 16, 21
Cremin, Lawrence: on informal education 3; on movies 3, 20

Deng, Xiaoping 91
Dewey, John 117
discourse 15, 16, 22
Dylan, Bob: *Blowin' in the Wind* 3
dynamic subordinancy 10

education: distinguished from learning 27–28; and racial justice 3; STEM (science, technology, engineering, math) 15–16
Education Education **42**, 43, 80, 86–88, **99**, **101**, 102, **103**, 105

Fenghuang Qin see *Country Teachers*
filmmaking: in China 3–4, 5–6, 7, 11, 15,
  17, 26, 27, 37, 40, 85, 93, 106;
  as leadership 6, 9, 12, 13, 14,
  20, 37, 55, 93, 108, 109, 118
Foss, Sonja K. 40

Gao, Xiaosong 105
Gao San see *Senior Year*
gugan jiaoshi 6, 118
guangbo ticao 85

He, Qun 6, 89–92
Hemphill, John K.: leadership categories
  14, 24, 55
High Noon 3, 47

Illich, Ivan 19

Jarvie, I. 109
Jiang, Mengjie 104
jiaoyu lingdao

King, Martin Luther 9

language 6, 12, 13, 32–34, 35, 120;
  Mandarin 5–6, 13, 32, 118
leadership: authority and 2, 5, 10, 11,
  20, 21–26; discursive 15,
  26; definitions of 13, 23, 24;
  dispensability of 30; as floating
  signifier 9, 22–23; leaders and
  4, 9, 15, 16–17, 21–22, 32; as
  natural human characteristic
  2, 12, 32, 118; power and 13,
  21–24; slippery nature of 9–10,
  21, 23, 118; tyranny and 13, 21;
  untethered 6, 13, 108, 118; as
  vector 2, 3, 13–15, 24, 27; zone
  of acceptance 24, 31, 31–32,
  60, 74
linguistics 12–13, 20, 32–34, 118
Lean on Me 10
Learning: formal and informal 27–29;
  parents and 16, 30, 31, 68; piano
  lessons 31; stamp collecting
  and 29
Lee, Yuan T. 14
Li, Keqiang 77
Li, Peng 92
lingdao: jiaoyu 3, 6, 10, 13; *lingdaoli* 6,
  12, 20, 116; *lingxiu* 9

Man who Shot Liberty Valance,
  The 5, 117
Mao, Zedong 9, 26
Mark of Youth **42**, **98**, **99**, **101**, **103**
"mavrickism" 10
Meili de Dajiao see *Pretty Big Feet*
mise-en-scene 37

Neuendorf, K. 44
Not One Less 6, 10, **42**, 72–79, 98, 100,
  101, **103**, 105, 109; actors 74;
  China Copyright Office and 78;
  fundraising impact 78–79; Li
  Keqiang and 77; social impact
  of 77–78

Ox-Bow Incident, The 3, 14

Picnic at Hanging Rock 4, 117
Please Vote for Me 17, 27, **42**, 79–86,
  88, 102; democracy and 80–81,
  84, 85, 102
power distance 11, 25, 32, 34
Pretty Big Feet 5, 34, 43, 45–53, 55–64,
  75, 76, 97, 99, 100, 101, 102,
  103, 104, 106, 108, 117
Public Broadcasting System (PBS) 67,
  79, 83

Race to Nowhere, The 16
Road, The 104
Road Home, The 73

School of Rock 10
school principals 2, 4, 5, 10, 20, 21, 22,
  25, 27, 30, 32, 66, 113, 116,
  117, 118
school reform 6, 14, 15, 66, 113, 118
Secondary School 64
Selznick, Phillip 9, 21
Senior Year 5, 42, 64–72, 80, 97, 99,
  102, 104, 108
Shining Teenagers 98
Shui Hu Zhuan 9
Simon, Paul 34
Singer, Irving 96
social harmony 11, 28
social media: surveys of usage
  110–111;
Solway, Clifford 36
Stewart, Jimmy 5, 117
suzhi jiaoyu 14, 81, 86

teachers 29, 30–32, 34, 89, 90–92; 97–100, 104, 113, 116, 117, 118, 119
Thomas, Ross: *As they are Portrayed: Principals in Film* 12, 116
To Sir with Love 4, 5, 10, 117
12 Angry Men 3, 13–14
12 Citizens 3
Two Million Minutes 16
tyranny 3, 13, 21

Why Democracy 79

Yang, Yazhou 52, 55
Yige Dou Buneng Shao see *Not One Less*

Zappa, Frank: *Trouble Comin' Every Day* 3
Zhang, Yimou 6, 73, 74–75, 76, 77–78
Zhou, Hao 64–65

For Product Safety Concerns and Information please contact our EU representative GPSR@taylorandfrancis.com
Taylor & Francis Verlag GmbH, Kaufingerstraße 24, 80331 München, Germany

www.ingramcontent.com/pod-product-compliance
Lightning Source LLC
Chambersburg PA
CBHW051754230426
43670CB00012B/2278